# RECORDS OF CIVILIZATION
## SOURCES AND STUDIES

*Edited under the auspices of the*

### DEPARTMENT OF HISTORY
#### COLUMBIA UNIVERSITY

---

---

## VOLUME XIII

## PEASANT LIFE IN OLD GERMAN EPICS

*From "Deutsche Literaturgeschichte," by Alfred Biese, by permission of C. H. Beck'sche Verlagsbuchhandlung.*

## HARTMANN VON AUE
From a miniature of the Weingartner Liederhandschrift.

# PEASANT LIFE
# IN OLD GERMAN EPICS

MEIER HELMBRECHT

AND

DER ARME HEINRICH

TRANSLATED FROM THE MIDDLE HIGH GERMAN
OF THE THIRTEENTH CENTURY

BY

## CLAIR HAYDEN BELL

ASSOCIATE PROFESSOR OF GERMAN, UNIVERSITY OF CALIFORNIA

NEW YORK

COLUMBIA UNIVERSITY PRESS

1931

Printed in the United States of America
The Torch Press, Cedar Rapids, Iowa

# PREFACE

Medieval writings which depict the life of humble folk are rare. The two thirteenth-century poems which are offered here in translation afford a glimpse of some of the more intimate aspects of life during that period. The one follows the career of a peasant boy who would play the knight; the other, employing the age-old theme of vicarious sacrifice, paints a picture, somewhat idealized, of the relations existing between a noble landowner and his dependent peasantry.

Although *Der arme Heinrich* was written earlier by some half century than *Meier Helmbrecht*, the latter poem is given first place in the following pages. This is not only because of its greater dramatic interest, but because it is, far more than *Der arme Heinrich*, a narrative of medieval German peasant life, and is thus more particularly the poem which justifies our title. It is, furthermore, of much greater value in its description of social conditions and in its cultural content in general.

The translations are based upon the texts as published in Panzer's fourth edition of *Meier Helmbrecht* and Gierach's edition of *Der arme Heinrich*. A long line of great poets and prose writers — Cowper, Ruskin, Newman, Wilhelm von Humboldt, Goethe — tell us that translation from one language to another, and particularly of verse, with full fidelity to both form and content, is impossible; that shipwreck must inevitably be suffered either on Scylla or in Charybdis. Both of these epics were written in the rhymed couplets that prevailed at the time, with four stresses to the line — a form which impresses us today as trying and monotonous; our ear is accustomed to an entirely different and freer flow of verse. We value these epics today for their content rather than for their formal beauty. And so I have made it my first endeavor to render faithfully the content of the poems. I may add, however, that I have sought to make a line for line rendering, with a verse-numbering identical with that of the German editions, a fact which enables easy reference to the originals. I shall be content if the translations, with all their limitations, prove to be of service to readers interested in this field, to whom the medieval language of the originals would constitute too great a deterrent.

The explanatory notes and the bibliography are placed at the end, where they will not annoy those who are not interested in them. The bibliography lists only the essential works under "General Literature"; otherwise it aims to be complete. It has seemed worth while to include such a bibliography here, since only fragmentary ones are available elsewhere. The arrangement under the various subdivisions of the bibliography is chronological, making it possible to observe the growth of interest in these works and to follow the critical discussion of them.

Obligation to the commentaries of European editors is acknowledged, and gratitude to friends who have offered suggestions. These translations, which were begun only as a pastime, would doubtless still be lying abandoned in a desk drawer but for the interest and counsel of Professors Austin P. Evans and Dana C. Munro. The former, who is the general editor of the series in which this volume appears, has afforded me guidance and constructive suggestion at every turn. More help than one may expect to receive even from the most generous colleague was given me, too, by my friend, Professor S. Griswold Morley, particularly with the translation of *Meier Helmbrecht*. To these good friends I express my cordial thanks.

C. H. B.

UNIVERSITY OF CALIFORNIA
June, 1931

# CONTENTS

# ILLUSTRATIONS

# INTRODUCTION

# INTRODUCTION

Two epic poems possessing unique value and interest stand out in the field of medieval German literature: Hartmann von Aue's *Der arme Heinrich* and Wernher der Gartenaere's *Meier Helmbrecht*. Although different in spirit and in substance, both treat of peasant life; both are rooted in German soil. They are the first unified, national stories, German in theme and in setting, developed in German literature.

*Meier Helmbrecht* is the greatest didactic satire produced in medieval Germany.[1] Unless we except *Der arme Heinrich*, which preceded it by some half-century, it is the first and only medieval German poem built on a consistent psychological basis, with the interest centered in character development rather than the march of events. The author consciously sets a psychological problem and solves it with astonishing directness and logical consistency. The Germanic scholar Franz Pfeiffer writes: "The German middle ages possess no second poem which might be placed at the side of this fresh, vigorous and gripping portrayal of folk life. How entirely different our literature would appear, what accomplishments its history would have to record, if this illustrious precedent . . . had awakened imitation!"[2] The other epic writers of the time sought their material in a remote, idealized past. Their aim was to entertain by the presentation of a series of motley adventures, strung together loosely on the thread of the narrative, shallow and conventional, bizarre and fantastic, borrowed for the most part from foreign sources, and bearing little imprint of national characteristics. The author of *Meier Helmbrecht* —

---

[1] A discussion of the author is found below, p. 13.

[2] Pfeiffer, "Forschung und Kritik," *Sitzungsberichte der philosophisch-historischen Classe der Kaiserlichen Akademie der Wissenschaften*, XLI (1863), 288-312.

3

the realist of the thirteenth century — set about, on the other hand, to relate something which he had seen "with his own eyes." Dipping into the fullness of life about him, he portrays the life and customs of his times in a poem which surpasses all others in medieval German literature in its value to the student of Germanic culture. He holds up a mirror where chivalry may behold its decay; the peasants, a grim warning against disloyalty to their class.

The splendor of knighthood had begun to pale early in the thirteenth century. More and more during the crusades and the wars in Italy men in the lower strata of knighthood rose into prominence, men of coarser strength and hardihood. Possessing no land, they found life carefree in time of war; in peace they had often to support themselves by plundering. An armed and mounted class, accustomed to war service, conscious of its power and difficult to hold in check, was a blessing only so long as its forces were directed toward some great and definite goal, such as the crusades and foreign wars had provided. The decline of the central power, the lack of foreign interests, the sinking of the ideals of knighthood, made this class an open menace to the safety of their own country. Within the empire the feuds, which even Kaiser Friedrich had not been able to subdue, gained the upper hand under his successors. The knight became a brigand, a brawling disturber of the peace, who stormed from one feud to another. Material want contributed greatly to the sinking of the noblest of the higher classes. Their affluence inevitably declined, because court life and the tournament consumed large sums. Economic superiority passed rapidly into the hands of the ascendant citizenry. From the middle of the thirteenth century the misuse of armed force became more and more prevalent; the tournaments, too, as Reinmar von Zweter remarks, became more *rinderlich* than *ritterlich*. Many an impoverished knight sought to improve his economic lot by taking a wife from the rich peasant class, for the sake of her money and land. Many a rich townsman and well-to-do peasant sought to win the title of knighthood; often money and land were sacrificed to this end. Men of the lower classes placed honor and life at stake

4

for the mere privilege of a place in the following of some robber knight who had built himself an impregnable nest on top of a hill or crag and scourged the surrounding country with his plundering sallies. It became difficult to distinguish knights from highwaymen, and the rich booty yielded by attacks upon town caravans was very tempting to the adventurous. There were stern laws permitting only knights to bear arms and forbidding townsmen and peasants under heavy penalty to carry them.[3] But pressure develops counter-pressure; how could these laws remain effective in turbulent times when self-protection was dictated by necessity? The peasant, like the townsman, was forced to arm himself in self-defense, even when wealth and vanity did not lead him thus to ape knightly fashion.

Concomitant with the sinking of knighthood and the rise of the citizen class, the beginnings of the thirteenth century had witnessed a rise in the social position of the peasant in the more favored localities; and from this time on, German literature displays a growing interest in him. The reason lies in his increasing affluence. His affectation and vanity, his conceit and his luxury in food and dress kept pace with his accumulating wealth and better standards of living. He cultivated foreign apparel, though its richness did not suffice to cloak the native crudeness of his manners, and merely made him the butt of jeering descriptions and caricature, awakening envy as a stimulant toward derisive literary treatment. When writers began to satirize the peasant, we may feel certain that the latter was living in comfortable, favorable circumstances. Bavaria and Austria, blessed by a bounteous nature and greater peace than other German territory, were the lands in which the peasant first struggled his way up to independence; consequently it is here that he first appears in literature. Along the fertile banks of the Danube the peasant cultivated acres that were free of debt and of heavy taxation. That the old man's sack was filled with money, the sons well knew! Because they were as well off as many a knight of the times, they strove to match the customs and dress of the latter. As Seifried Helbling derisively remarks,

---

[3] Landfrieden of 1256. Cf. Hügli, *Der deutsche Bauer im Mittelalter*, pp. 53 f.

5

Do something that the monkeys see,
They'll think it good and follow thee.[4]

In dress above all, this aping tendency most plainly revealed itself. Little heed was paid by the young peasant fops to the laws which prescribed plain cloth and monotonous gray or brown colors for their wear.[5] They sought in every way not only to equal but to outdo their models. They wore their hair in long, flowing curls. They devoted much care to the head-dress, a hood finely embroidered with designs in silk. The jacket was sewn with silk, ornamented with long rows of buttons of many colors, and buckled with a velvet belt. Trousers were to be seen which required sixteen yards of cloth for the making. Their red leather shoes came to a point and were embroidered with silk. Despite all edicts against a peasant's bearing arms, they carried swords and knives at their belts, and spears in their gloved hands. Spurs, to which bells were sometimes tied, clanked at their heels. They even wore breast-plates and helmets. Neidhart describes a young peasant whose dress was made up of twenty-four different kinds of cloth. Further interesting bits of description have been gleaned from Neidhart's poems by McLaughlin:

Perhaps you would like to hear how the rustics are dressed. Their clothes are above their place. Small coats they wear, and small cloaks; red hoods, shoes with buckles, and black hose. They have on silk pouch-bags, and in them they carry pieces of ginger, to make themselves agreeable to the girls. They wear their hair long — a privilege of good birth. They put on gloves that come up to their elbows. One appears in a fustian jacket green as grass. Another flaunts it in red. Another carries a sword long as a hemp flail, wherever he goes; the knob of its hilt has a mirror, that he makes the girls look at themselves in. Poor clumsy louts, how can the girls endure them? One of them tears his partner's veil, another sticks his sword hilt through her gown, as they are dancing, and more than once, enthusiastically dancing and excited by the music, their awkward feet tread on the girls' skirts and even drag them off. But they

---

[4] *Der kleine Lucidarius* (Seifried Helbling), 1, 453.
[5] These laws are first mentioned in the *Kaiserchronik*, by Pfaffe Konrad, 1147, ed. E. Schröder, Hannover, 1892. Cf. Hügli, *op. cit.*, pp. 32-34.

are more than clumsy, they have an offensive horse-play that is nothing less than insult.[6]

From such descriptions it is clear that Wernher's account of Helmbrecht's garb, although it involves exaggeration, is in the main a realistic description.

The literature of the thirteenth century contains sufficient descriptions of the half knight, half peasant type to convince us that this class was common in the social life of the period. Knighthood was no longer conferred solely in recognition of deeds of valor performed on the field of honor, but was now extended also to townsman and peasant for services rendered. The more successful peasants bound less successful fellow-peasants to themselves in a servile relation. Through years of trust and service, vassals rose from serfdom to associate on intimate terms with their lords. These *Ministerialen*,[7] as they are called, were given fiefs, wore the coat of arms of their *seigneur*, and sometimes, as in the case of Hartmann von Aue, also bore his noble family name. Thus there arose in the course of a century a new nobility alongside the old, embracing within its ranks members from all strata of society.

The impoverishment of the nobility and the ascendancy of the peasant are described fully in *Der kleine Lucidarius* (Seifried Helbling).[8] Here the peasant wins favor of a nobleman by his service as a lower official or manager. He sends his son to court, and his daughters sew for the court ladies. His son marries one of the nobleman's daughters; the nobleman's son marries the rich daughter of the peasant official. The descendants of the marriages are dubbed knights. The land that the former peasant rented from the nobleman, he now receives in knightly fief. Similar accounts are given by the poet Hugo von Trimberg in his *Renner*:[9] A young peasant, carrying his first sword, bears himself proudly and sings to the girls at the dance. His admiring mother talks of him to a nobleman's

---

[6] McLaughlin, *Studies in Medieval Life and Literature*, p. 91.

[7] *Dienstleute*, servitors.

[8] This poem dates from between the years 1283 and 1299. Ed. by J. Seemüller, Halle, 1886.

[9] A poem of about the year 1300. Ed. by the Bamberg Historischer Verein, 1833-1836.

squire, who thereupon tells her that he knows where so promising a youth can find just the right wife. Sorely needing oats for his horse and food for himself, he receives these in abundance, and then

> Rides back home to Hungerdale,
> Where goods as well as honor fail.
>
> Vss. 1605 f.

In the castle the dancing mice find it necessary to forage elsewhere to satisfy their hunger. The peasant wife brings further gifts of food to the squire; peasant and son likewise call. Opportunity beckons: the son marries the knight's daughter, decked out in her begged, ill-fitting finery. The offspring are *parvenus*, by name and occupation related to Helmbrecht Schlingdasgeu and his comrades, whom we meet in the poem to follow. These are the social conditions which form the background for the story told us in *Meier Helmbrecht*. From the mouth of the old peasant we hear the bitter complaint, raised so generally by the poets of the thirteenth century, over the decay of knighthood and the lapse of court etiquette. Peasant Helmbrecht's son is a typical well-to-do fop such as has been described, who from vanity and love of adventure, as well as from repugnance to farm work, joins the retinue of a robber knight.

About two hundred years passed, after the composing of this poem, before it was recorded in the older of the two manuscripts still extant. This is the Berlin MS B, written in Austria in the fifteenth century. The younger MS A is a part of the Ambras Heldenbuch that Kaiser Maximilian, called "the last knight," a zealous collector of the cultural documents of knighthood, caused to be written down in the years 1504 to 1515 by one Hans Ried. These two manuscripts vary considerably from each other in their text, although they were apparently transcribed from a common source. Hans Ried was by far the more faithful copyist; the older copyist, as MS B betrays,[10] made many changes according to his impulse, both in content and in form. Hence MS A is throughout much

---

[10] Cf. Panzer, *Meier Helmbrecht*, p. ix.

8

the more reliable of the two, needing correction from B only in rare instances.

An important difference in the two manuscripts lies in the locality given as the scene of the action. In connection with a description of Helmbrecht's costume, we are assured in verses 191 f.:

> No peasant wore such costly work
> Twixt Hohenstein and Haldenberk.

The less reliable copyist gives instead of these place names: *zwuschen Wels und dem Traunberg*. Again, in verses 896 ff., where Meier Helmbrecht praises the spring water which he offers to his son, MS A reads:

> No equally good spring I know
> Except the Wanghaus spring so clear,
> But no one brings its waters here.

For *Wanchhûsen*, MS B gives *Leubenbach* (present-day Leonbach).[11] If, then, we may trust the more reliable Ambras manuscript, the place of action lies in Upper Austria, south of the confluence of the Salzach with the River Inn, a region which until the eighteenth century belonged to Bavaria. The region indicated in MS B is likewise in Upper Austria, lying somewhat further to the east.

There is but one place known by the name of Wanghausen, and its mention afforded the best starting point for determining the locality in which the action occurs. It lies on the east side of the Salzach, in Austria, opposite the Bavarian hamlet Burghausen. There is today still a spring in Wanghausen which, because of the excellent water it furnishes, is called by the native folk *das goldene Brünnlein*. A minute study of the surrounding territory has been made by Friedrich Keinz, followed later by L. Fulda and M. Schlickinger. The results of this investigation are most interesting. Having discovered a Helmbrecht Farm in legal records of the thirteenth century,

---

[11] Chance has revealed the probable motive which led the scribe of MS B to alter the place names: that he might do honor to his patron, Lienhart Mewrll, who was owner of Leubenbach at the time. Cf. Panzer, *Meier Helmbrecht*, p. ix; and "Zum Meier Helmbrecht," *Btr* XXVII (1902), 88-112.

Keinz succeeded in locating the actual farm in the neighborhood of Wanghausen, some six kilometers east of Burghausen on the edge of the Weilhart forest. This holding was up to the last century called the *Helmbrechtshof*. Even for the peasant Ruprecht of the poem, documentary record of a contemporary, Ruperth von Schitir, has been found. The farms *Schiderer* and *Groszschieder* which lie southeast of the Helmbrecht farm may have been his holdings. Near at hand is the Reuter spring, the only one in the region with good water, justifying father Helmbrecht's comparison of it with the Wanghausen spring. *Hohenstein* is the Hohenberg, near Burghausen, and *Haldenberg* is perhaps identical with the hill Adenberg, lying not far away in the opposite direction from the Helmbrecht farm. Near the farm there stretches a forest such as is featured in the poem, the Weilhart. At a distance of about an hour's walk, in the midst of this forest, there stands a huge linden tree of a hoary old age, and under it a little chapel, the *Weisse Schacher*, concerning which Keinz found a legend still in circulation among the peasant folk, that it marks the spot where a soldier who had run away from his parents in order to lead a dissolute life was once hanged. As the decades and centuries passed after the disappearance of knights, popular tradition may easily have changed the follower of the robber knight into a soldier. The chapel as it now stands dates from a later time than that of the poem; yet it is not improbable that relatives of the hanged man originally constructed the chapel, inviting passers-by to say a paternoster for the salvation of the sinner on the spot of his execution. Many of the unusual expressions occurring in the poem have found explanation in the language and customs of the region studied. One of the investigators found in 1865 an old peasant, Lindl, who recollected that in his youth he had seen in the nearby monastery Ranshofen (abandoned in 1811) a book, with illustrations, about a "robber chieftain Helm" from Gilgenberg.

Some of the matters above mentioned are established fact. Much is only hypothesis. Critics however generally accept the view that the actual scene of the action of Wernher's poem has been successfully identified, and that a substratum of historical fact underlies the narrative. Thus Wernher's assertions that he was telling at first hand a story of actual events may well be true.[12] To point out that the poet has fashioned his tale with the free hand of a creative artist need not necessarily cast discredit upon the poem's historical basis. It is evident from the literary character of the epic that it is not in every detail historical. There is even evidence of direct literary influence which, if it did not suggest the entire story, at least furnished Wernher with a general *motif*, and inspired him to treat an event from the field of his own experience in the light of a given model.

The singer Neidhart von Reuenthal, who preceded Wernher,[13] busied himself in his village lyrics, as we have seen, with the same *milieu* as that which is reflected in the *Meier Helmbrecht*. One has to read but few of Neidhart's songs to discover numerous analogies with Wernher's poem. There is the same general satirical treatment. One meets the same vain peasant youths, who strive to imitate the knights. There are the frivolous peasant girls who consider it an honor to yield themselves to a man of higher degree. It is apparent that Wernher must have been thoroughly familiar with Neidhart's songs. Specific proof of the relationship is furnished in the glowing tribute which Wernher pays to Neidhart, amounting almost to an acknowledgment of indebtedness.[14] Last, and perhaps most convincing evidence of all, there are the stanzas in which Neidhart, describing a young peasant named Hildemar, furnishes in brief almost an entire exposition of the Helmbrecht plot. Translated into English, these read:

On his head a hood he wears, drawn tight with strings inside it,
Pretty birds in brightest silk worked on it round about.
More than one swift-moving hand has deft with fingers plied it,
Ere they thus embroidered it; this fact you need not doubt.
He must bear my curses wroth

---

[12] Panzer, Schiffmann and Braune are the leading critics in opposition to this view.

[13] The dates of Neidhart's birth and death are unknown. His poetic activity falls between 1180 and 1250.    [14] Vss. 217 ff.

Who conceived and thought it,
Who abroad the silk and cloth
Bought, and hither brought it.

Have you ne'er beheld his locks, so curled and long and shining?
Down around his chin they fall, in thick and close array.
In the hood they lie of nights, held shapely by confining,
Blond and fine like richest silk, as soft in every way.
From the tying, well 'tis curled
Where the hood confines it.
Like a mane it flows unfurled
Where no tying binds it.

Brazen, he would be the peer of men of high degree,
Who at court have spent their days and there from youth have grown.
His hood, if once they catch him, will be stripped off speedily;
Ere he knows what's happened him, his birds will all have flown.
Let such reward as he'll receive
Be his ambition's yield.
Many a youth, you may believe,
Like wild, now roams the field.

There is a similarity of detail here which cannot be acci-
dental, even to the scattering of the birds on the hood.[15] We
note, however, the important difference that in Neidhart's
prophecy Hildemar will be driven away in shame and disgrace
by the court people whom he apes, while Wernher's Helmbrecht suffers death at the hands of his own kind whom he has
misused. Neidhart's influence upon Wernher is universally
recognized. But it must be borne in mind that the two poets
knew the same peasants, of the same epoch. Wernher's frank
reference to Neidhart is not that of a poet who seeks to hide
his literary borrowing. It is, on the other hand, an acknowl-
edgement of the relation of his character Helmbrecht to those
pictured by Neidhart. The type was common; but, as Meyer
aptly says,[16] Wernher has not had to undress Hildemar in
order to bedeck his Helmbrecht. Furthermore, Wernher has
many guides other than Neidhart. It has been shown that, if

---

[15] Cf. Wiessner, "Helmbrecht und Neidharts Strophen über Hildemar," *Btr*
XLIX (1924), 152 ff.
[16] Meyer, "Helmbrecht und seine Haube," *ZfdPh* XL (1908), 426.

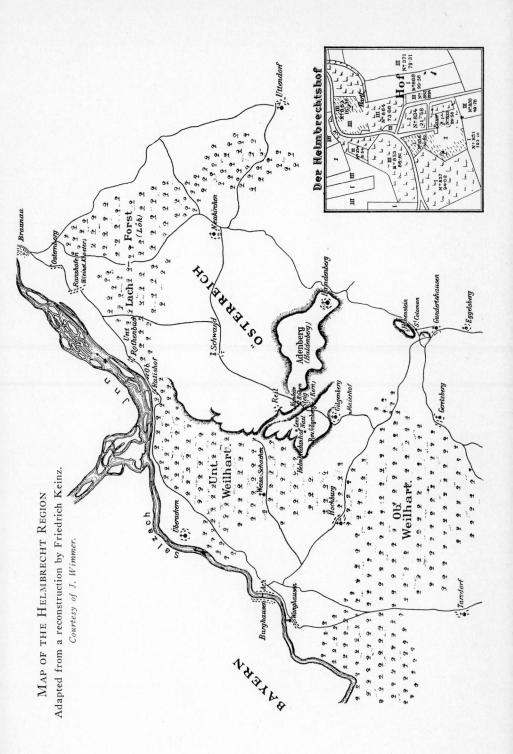

MAP OF THE HELMBRECHT REGION

Adapted from a reconstruction by Friedrich Keinz.

*Courtesy of J. Wimmer.*

Wernher's world was that of Neidhart, he saw this world largely through the eyes of Wolfram von Eschenbach; and his poem contains reminiscences of Hartmann von Aue, Stricker, Freidank, Walther von der Vogelweide, and the folk epics.[17]

As for the author whom we have to thank for our narrative, we have no positive knowledge whatever save the fragment of information which he gives us in the last line of his poem; here he announces his identity as Wernher der Gartenaere, a name not recorded elsewhere. All else is more or less uncertain inference, based upon the nature and contents of the poem. C. Schröder has sought to identify the author with Bruder Wernher, an Austrian writer of aphorisms whose activity can be traced from 1217 to 1250.[18] But there is nothing beyond the partial similarity of names to justify the hypothesis; viewpoint, language and technique of the two poets are so divergent as to make this identification unacceptable.[19] The language of the poem indicates either Bavarian or Austrian origin. Keinz's theory, that Wernher was a "pater" gardener in the Augustinian monastery Ranshofen which stood some two hours' distance north of the Helmbrecht farm, has found considerable favor. This "pater" gardener, so runs Keinz's theory, not only supervised the extensive agricultural holdings of the monastery, but also instructed the peasants of the region in the arts of horticulture. In line with this duty, he was called upon to travel about from farm to farm, and in this close contact with the folk life in which the Helmbrecht story has its setting, he may have witnessed the events of the story at first hand or have heard them from the peasants of the region. This would also explain the poet's thorough and detailed familiarity with the geography of the locality in which the action takes place. He knew the region on the lower Inn River so minutely that he must either have grown up there or have dwelt there long in later life.

Friedrich Panzer, whose widely used edition of *Meier Helmbrecht* has been followed in our translation, opposes the

---

[17] Pfannmüller, "Meier Helmbrecht," *Btr* XL (1918), 252 ff.

[18] Schröder, "Bruder Wernher," *Ergänzungsblätter zur Kenntniss der Gegenwart*, III (1869).      [19] Panzer, *Meier Helmbrecht*, p. x, note 2.

Keinz hypothesis on the basis of internal evidence in the poem.[20] The lines (vss. 780 f.)

> And only barest dues alone
> Shall priest or monk receive from me,

Panzer considers impossible from a monk, while Keinz interprets them in connection with verse 256 as referring to the tithe which the elder Helmbrecht paid yearly, in produce, to the neighboring monastery. Realistic writer as he was, Wernher would certainly picture the attitude of the average peasant to this degree of accuracy.[21] Panzer points out also the sally against the nuns in 109 ff., and against the donations to the nun in 125 ff. And the remark made in 208 ff., where the poet speaks of himself as a dancer, is difficult to explain as coming from the pen of a monastery inmate. One of the most weighty bits of evidence is afforded by verses 848 ff.:

> Much as I've wandered through the land,
> Such kindly care I've nowhere had
> As was bestowed upon this lad.

While the Keinz hypothesis interprets this travel as having occurred in connection with the "pater" gardener's duties in supervision of the horticultural activities in the lands surrounding the monastery, Panzer considers it to be clear evidence that the poet was a wandering minstrel, who moved from court to court to ply his art and thereby gain his bread. The significance of Wernher's cognomen *der gartenaere* would then remain hidden to us. Pfeiffer seeks to derive the appellative from a rare Bavarian verb *garten, to wander about from house to house*; although for such derivation we should expect the form *gartaere* rather than *gartenaere*.[22] Schiffmann has pointed out a noble family in Krems on the Danube by the name of Gartner (<*gartenaere*). The existence of this family is documented since 1293, and Wernher's membership in it would afford an

---

[20] *Ibid.*, pp. xi ff.

[21] Cf. Gough, "The Authorship of . . . Meier Helmbrecht," *Proceedings of the Leeds Philos. and Lit. Society*, Literary and Historical Section I, Pt. 2 (1926), 56.

[22] Panzer, *Meier Helmbrecht*, p. xiv, note 1.

explanation of the unusual surname.[23] Schiffmann's suggestion would make of Wernher a nobleman. Even the class from which he originated cannot be inferred with certainty. He expressly calls himself a "poet" in verse 1933, but was he by birth a knight, or had he sprung from the peasant class?

Wernher would surely have aroused ringing applause with the recital of his tale under the village linden tree. However Panzer and those who see in Wernher a wandering minstrel hold that he plied his art at the courts of nobility. His poem is conceived much in the style of his forerunner, the court singer Neidhart. He pictures young Helmbrecht in Neidhart's spirit of satire, and his verses 913 ff., so argues Panzer, are addressed specifically to the nobility.[24] Karl Stechele, of Burghausen,[25] has set up the hypothesis that the poet was a certain Sir Wernher, known to have been in the following of the dukes of Bavaria, resident at Burghausen, and that in the latter part of his life this knight entered the neighboring monastery, where he made himself useful as head gardener. The name of a Sir Wernher of Burghausen appears as a witness in a document of the monastery Ranshofen in 1210, and there is further documentary evidence that he and his son of the same name were present at Ranshofen in 1215. Stechele presents a fairly convincing argument, and one that meets most of Panzer's difficulties. But, on the other hand, one must not overlook Wernher's explicit denial of his high standing in verse 864,

---

[23] Schiffmann, "Studien zum Helmbrecht," *Btr* XLII (1917), 13 f.

[24] Panzer, *Meier Helmbrecht*, p. xiii: "Darüber kann kein Zweifel sein, dass er seine Kunst nicht unter der Dorflinde, sondern am Hofe geübt hat. Vom Standpunkte des Hofes und für den Hof hat er sein Gedicht verfasst und ganz im Stile Neidharts verspottet er seinen dörperlichen Helden. Die V. 913 ff. sind durchaus an den Adel gerichtet." But cf. Gough, "The Authorship of . . . Meier Helmbrecht," *loc. cit.*, p. 55: "I cannot conceive, with Panzer, that the poem was written for the entertainment of courts. The description (1020-1035) of the debased chivalry of the time would not be pleasant hearing to the knights — if intended for such. No *Fahrender* would have dared to speak so openly, in fact nobody but a cleric protected by the sanctity of his calling." And Haertel, "Social Conditions in Southern Bavaria," *Trans. of the Wisconsin Acad. of Sciences, Arts, and Letters*, XVII (1914), 1058: "The complaints against knighthood . . . would, at the very least, cause the expulsion of the guilty poet from the castle."

[25] Stechele, "In des Herzogs Stube auf der Burg zu Burghausen," *Das Bayerland*, XXXIII (1921-22), 344-349.

where he speaks of himself as being no *herre in hôher aht* (lord in high esteem) ; and his remark in verses 884 f., "Such food would surely please a lord," seems that of a person not himself of noble rank. Moreover, despite the strong influence of Neidhart mentioned above, the poem taken as a whole has a flavor distinctly different from that of court poetry. Wernher shows a remarkable familiarity with the life and mental horizon of the peasant, and has created in the older Helmbrecht a more sympathetic character and one of more dignity and nobility of thought than could well have come from the pen of a knight. Neidhart was envious of his peasants, quarrelled with them, and as a nobleman born looked down upon them with scorn. Wernher is more detached in his views; he severely arraigns knights and peasants alike for the evil conditions that prevail among them. He has no quarrel with the upright peasant; he shows for him rather such a benevolent sympathy and so high a regard for the value of his calling, that his attitude arrests our attention.

Coulton remarks in his *Medieval Village*,[26] "in all medieval literature, the peasant is very seldom noticed, and, even then, the notice is universally scornful." The peasant was in a sense the pariah of medieval society, ordained by God to labor by the sweat of his brow and looked down upon as a "necessary domestic beast." [27] The clerical group as well as the nobility shared in this contemptuous view of the laboring class. As for the peasant himself, he produced no literature, consequently he never spoke for himself.[28] The importance that attaches to Wernher's view of the peasant becomes apparent when we observe the rarity of such a favorable attitude. Coulton remarks, with considerable exaggeration, that in the entire field of medieval literature this poem and *Piers Plowman* are the two exceptions to the universal scorn, standing out altogether unparalleled for the sympathy they express for peasant life.[29] Wernher's sympathetic attitude, amounting almost to "class consciousness," may indicate that he himself came from

---

[26] Page 237.  [27] Coulton, *Medieval Village*, p. 234.

[28] Hügli, *Der deutsche Bauer im Mittelalter*, p. 1.

[29] Coulton, *Medieval Village*, p. 237. That this is an overstatement appears

16

peasant stock and looked back upon the occupation of farming with affection.[30] However that may be, it seems safe to infer that he was a cleric. There are not only the author's love of poetry and his familiarity with the literature of his time, but also his acquaintance with current Latin farces dealing with the home-coming of the scholar, from which Wernher borrowed in his treatment of Helmbrecht's first home-coming,[31] and his acquaintance perhaps with the *Iliad* and the *Aeneid*.[32] More convincing, however, than these details is the mere fact of the presentation of a peasant thus early in so strongly favorable a light. The clerics may have been, on the whole, as Coulton maintains, scornful and contemptuous of the peasant and his lot, yet it is among the churchmen that we find the expression of a more sympathetic attitude.[33] Christ, it will be remembered, called his Father a husbandman,[34] and Christians are enjoined in Ecclesiastes vii, 16: "Hate not laborious works, nor husbandry enjoined by the Most High." Religious parables which are based upon agriculture are very numerous. Thus we find the great medieval German preacher, Berchtold von Regensburg, likening Christianity to a field, the treasures of the soil to souls, and God himself to the plowman who plows the field with the cross.[35] Such figures of speech had the young peasant maiden in *Der arme Heinrich* heard from the priests, that led her to say, in declaring her purpose to die for her beloved lord, Herr Heinrich:

> A farmer seeks me for his wife
> To whom I gladly yield my life.
> O, give me to him then, betide,
> And all my wants will be supplied.

from the fact that in the other poem contained in this volume, *Der arme Heinrich*, we also find a peasant presented as an ideal character. And it is worth observation that a strong monkish influence prevails in Hartmann's poem.

[30] Haertel's view, "that Wernher was an intelligent old peasant living in the comfortable circumstances described in his poem," impresses us as having small plausibility indeed. "Social Conditions in Southern Bavaria," *loc. cit.*, p. 1059.

[31] Panzer, "Zum Meier Helmbrecht," *Btr* XXXIII (1908), 393 ff.

[32] See *infra*, note 3 to *Meier Helmbrecht*, and Meyer, "Helmbrecht und seine Haube," *loc. cit.*, p. 428.

[33] Coulton, *Medieval Village*, p. 230.     [34] John xv, 1.

[35] Berchtold von Regensburg, *Deutsche Predigten*, ed. Pfeiffer, I, 357 f.

17

His plow moves steadily indeed,
His yard is stored for every need.
His horses, cattle, never die,
With him, the children never cry, etc.

Vss. 775 ff.

The Church, then, viewed the lot of the peasant as ordained by God, and sought to encourage him in his toil by representing labor as an essential condition of life, and by pointing out the importance to society of his work as the creator of bread. In his chapter, "Church Estimates of the Peasant," [36] in which Coulton asserts: "Nearly all our full-length pictures of the medieval peasant come from churchmen; but these are preponderantly unfavorable," he also concedes:[37] "It is true that Christianity did something real . . . for the ennobling of manual labor." Hügli shows how under the influence of Christian teaching the attitude toward labor gradually changed in Germany, until toward the end of the thirteenth century we find German monks pronouncing the peasant to be the beloved child of God because of his ceaseless toil, which is pleasing to him.[38] Whether the peasant himself, in the sweat of his toil, felt himself to be so beloved of God and took such pride in his work, is another question.[39]

---

[36] Coulton, *Medieval Village*, pp. 231-252; see p. 242 for quotation.

[37] *Ibid.*, p. 233.      [38] Hügli, *Der deutsche Bauer im Mittelalter*, pp. 64-66.

[39] Self-possessed pride in occupation such as Farmer Helmbrecht utters (vss. 545 ff.) found expression and has come down to us in an old folk-song, *Ritter und Bauer*, which Uhland has recorded in his *Alte hoch- und niederdeutsche Volkslieder*, I, 337. It reads in part, in prose translation: "(2) The knight said: 'I am by birth of noble race.' The peasant said: 'I grow grain; that, methinks, is far better. You'd soon have to forget your nobility if it were not for my farming. I feed you from the furrows of my plow, if you will credit me for it. . . . (4) I do not give as much as a bit of chaff for your courtly doings. The customs of my agricultural pursuit, methinks, are better. Of what good is your lance-tilting and your dancing? I see no good in them. My hard labor is sound, and the world profits by it.'"

Old poems of the peasantry which express similar sentiment may be found in Johannes Bolte's collection: *Der Bauer im deutschen Liede*, 32 Lieder des 15.-19. Jahrhunderts (Berlin, 1890), *Acta Germanica*, I, 173-308. All of these folk-songs, however, are some two centuries later in origin than *Meier Helmbrecht*, and come from a period in which the opposition between peasant and knight was much more deeply and sharply felt than in the thirteenth century. Cf Hügli, *Der deutsche Bauer im Mittelalter*, p. 66.

18

It is from the clerical class, then, that the sympathetic attitude shown toward the peasant in *Meier Helmbrecht* might be expected. Gough, although rejecting Keinz's theory that Wernher was a "pater" gardener,[40] presents the hypothesis that he was a wandering member of the Franciscan Order. He points out what may be regarded as Franciscan characteristics in the speech which Wernher puts into the mouth of the old Meier, and he somewhat convincingly argues away the difficulties which have been raised against the monk theory. Certainty upon this point, however, cannot be attained: we must rest content that for the present at least there is not sufficient evidence in hand to decide the matter. Wernher may possibly have been a knight or a wandering minstrel; more likely he was an itinerant monk, or even, as Keinz argues, a "pater" gardener.

The precise date at which *Meier Helmbrecht* was written remains undetermined. The most definite clue is given by the author in verse 217, where the poet Neidhart von Reuenthal is referred to as already dead. The year of Neidhart's death is unfortunately not known. His last poem which can be definitely dated was written in 1236. Again, in verse 728, Helmbrecht affects an aristocratic tone by use of a Bohemian greeting. The practice of embellishing one's speech with Bohemian words could hardly have gained vogue until after the coming of Bohemian supremacy in Austria in 1246.[41] Verse 411, with its reference to the "Kaiser," has been thought to cast some light upon the problem. The last emperor before the Great Interregnum was Friedrich II, who was deposed in 1245 and died in 1250. The argument has been advanced that the title would hardly have been thus used after 1250, in a period when the enthroning of a new German emperor could not be foreseen; this inference is unsound, as the title may well have been used without reference to an individual, merely connoting the greatest temporal power. The *terminus ad quem* is set by the fact

---

[40] Gough's rejection ("The Authorship of . . . Meier Helmbrecht," *loc. cit.*, p. 52) is based solely upon an argument advanced by Schiffmann relative to the meaning of the M.H.G. word *scherge*, but this argument has been entirely refuted. Cf. *infra*, note to *Meier Helmbrecht*, No. 54.

[41] Cf. E. Schröder, review of Seemüller, "Studien zum kleinen Lucidarius," *AfdA* X (1884), 56-58.

that Pleyer, the Salzburg poet, has been influenced by *Meier Helmbrecht* (about 1260); such influence is even more unmistakable in the work of Seifried Helbling, an Austrian poet who can be traced from the year 1282 to 1299. The first definite allusion in literature to *Helmbrecht* is to be found in Ottokar's *Rheimchronik* (about 1310), where certain peasants, in refusing military service, appeal as their justification to the teachings of father Helmbrecht.[42] These bits of evidence set the date of our poem at about the middle of the thirteenth century.

It would appear that the poem did not become known far beyond the confines of its home region. Neither it nor its author won the mention of contemporary poets, such as was commonly given to court singers, and such as Wernher himself accords to Neidhart.[43] To the folk of his native region the contents of the poem, or the events upon which it was based, were doubtless well known; Keinz tells us that in popular parlance the word *Helmbrecht* was used to designate any frivolous or wild person. There is even evidence that in this sense the word passed over into Bohemian: the Czech philosopher Štitný in the fourteenth century uses the masculine word *helmbrecht* as a common substantive with the meaning *libertine*, a feminine derivative *helmbrechtice* (loose woman), and the adjective *helmbrechtny* (dissolute).[44]

With the complete decay of chivalry at the end of the fourteenth and in the fifteenth century this poem, too, sank into oblivion until, under the spur of the interest awakened by Romanticism, scholars of the nineteenth century unearthed it with other gems of the past and restored it to the German people. Of the two manuscripts extant, the Germanic scholar Bergmann published one in 1839, and F. H. von der Hagen the other in 1850. Since that time numerous critical editions have appeared. Yet not the scholar alone finds merit in this unique poem: popular interest is shown in the appearance of

---

[42] 26, 417 f.: *Helmbrechtes vater lêre wil ich gerne volgen und der kneppischeit sin erbolgen.* Attention was first called to this passage by Haupt, "Kleine Bermerkungen, 2," *ZfdA* III (1843), 279.

[43] Vs. 217.      [44] Lambel, *Meier Helmbrecht*, p. 139.

some fourteen renderings in modern German verse and numerous prose versions. Of the former, the best are by Ludwig Fulda and Johann Pilz. Among the latter, Josef Hofmiller, writing in a pithy, forceful vernacular, has created an enduring work of art. And Ortner, in his recent three-act tragedy *Meier Helmbrecht* has gripped present-day audiences with this stirring thirteenth-century epic, recast in dramatic form.[45]

Although, as is generally acknowledged, Wernher drew inspiration from Neidhart, he far surpassed his teacher. Both in form and in material he struck out upon a path unknown to the epic writers of his time. His realistic detail makes of the poem a veritable mine for treasure-seekers in the field of cultural history.[46] From the standpoint of literature, one must of course not expect this medieval poet to have at his command the technique of present-day writers. Wernher's exposition is too long, and the dialogue, more than half of the poem, is extended in entire disproportion to the length of the action. Nevertheless, in the picture he gives us of the social life of his times, in the dramatic intensity of his plot, and in the opposition between the older and the younger generation, representing the eternally conflicting elements of the old and the new, he has created a work of lasting interest and of universal significance.

Both peasant and knight, as we have seen, appear in *Meier Helmbrecht*. Both appear likewise in Hartmann's *Der arme Heinrich*, which, as has been stated above, preceded Wernher's poem by some half century. While in *Meier Helmbrecht* there is a strong breath of discord and opposition between the two classes, the earlier poem pictures the knight and his dependent peasantry in a relationship of happy, idyllic harmony and accord.

It is surprising that so little is definitely known of the life of a poet whose works were so renowned as those of Hartmann von Aue. As is the case with Wernher, no direct documentary

---

[45] Complete data will be found in the Bibliography, pp. 155 ff.

[46] As an illustration of the wealth of such detail, an analysis of the poem for the light it casts upon the peasant's food will be found in the Appendix, pp. 149 ff.

testimony concerning him has come down to us, so that nearly all that we know of him is what we can glean from his writings, together with such comments upon him as were made by contemporary poets.

Hartmann names himself for us in most of his works, and in the introduction of *Der arme Heinrich* he informs us of his station in life:

> A knight there was — so learned he,
> That he could read quite easily
> In manuscripts and books; the same
> Hartmann von Ouwe was by name;
> He served at Ouwe in vassalage.
>
> Vss. 1 ff.

He was, then, a knight, probably of a poor family, in the service of the lord of Ouwe. This *Ouwe* (modern *Aue* or *Au*: *meadow*) is a place name of frequent occurrence, both alone and in compounds, and it is not surprising that its location should be contested. There are three places of this name that come into consideration: (1) Obernau, near Rottenburg on the Neckar; (2) Aue, or Ortenau, in the Breisgau, some few miles south of Freiburg; and (3) Eglisau, formerly Ouwe, on the Rhine in Switzerland.[47]

It is a well established fact that Hartmann was a Swabian. He tells us in *Der arme Heinrich* that the Herr Heinrich of whom he writes and whose family he served was resident in Swabia.[48] Hartmann's high praise of the Swabians in verses 1420 ff. of the same poem likewise points in this direction. The contemporary poet Heinrich von dem Türlin makes specific reference to Hartmann as a Swabian poet. And the evidence afforded by these passages is abundantly supported by the language of Hartmann's works.

The poet's literary activity falls in the last decade of the twelfth and the first decade of the thirteenth century. He was born about 1170. As a boy he apparently entered a monastery school and received an education far superior to that commonly enjoyed by those of his class. He became familiar with

---

[47] Ehrismann, *Geschichte der deutschen Literatur*, p. 142.    [48] Vs. 31.

the Bible, learned to read Latin, and came to know the Roman poets. In order to fit himself for his knightly calling, he left this school, presumably about the age of fifteen, and acquired all the accomplishments of knighthood. The influence of his clerical schooling followed him, however, throughout his life, and affected greatly his moral views and his writings. A trip to France added the final polish to his education; there he learned the French language and became familiar with French literature, from which he was later to borrow.

The first products of Hartmann's pen were love lyrics. In accordance with the requirements of knightly custom he wrote a number of *Minnesongs*, and a longer poem, *Das Büchlein*, in honor of a lady. Yet his chief accomplishment lies in the field of the epic. Of his epics, two, *Erec* and *Iwein*, belong to profane literature, while the other two, *Gregorius auf dem Steine* and *Der arme Heinrich*, are legends of religious cast. The dates of these epics cannot be set with certainty. *Erec* was written about 1192, *Iwein* about 1202. Somewhere between them fall *Gregorius* and *Der arme Heinrich*. The date of the latter poem cannot be set more accurately than at the dividing line of the two centuries.[49]

Little further light is shed upon Hartmann's career by his writings. Between knightly activities and literary occupation his life would seem to have flowed evenly, with little of great fortune or of misfortune to mark it. One event moved him to the depths of his heart — the death of his master, to whom he bore a remarkable loyalty and devotion, the loyalty of the ideal vassal to his lord. Of this event he writes:

> Since death has stricken down with cruel hand
> My master, know
> That I no longer care how matters stand
> Down here below.
>
> How happiness dies out with him! And how
> My joy all went!
> Upon the soul's eternal welfare now
> My thoughts are bent.

---

[49] Ehrismann, *op. cit.*, p. 146; cf. Sparnay, "Die Einstellung des Armen Heinrichs . . .," *ZfdA* LXVII (1930), 23-41.

And can it aid his soul in anything
That service to the cross I now shall bring,
May half of my reward become his own,
And may I see him soon before God's throne.

Riding forth on the crusade of 1197, Hartmann bids farewell not only to his homeland but also to *Minnedienst*, intent
now upon devoting himself to *Gottesminne*. He probably
returned from this crusade in the spring of the following
year. He was still living and writing in the beginning of the
thirteenth century. Gottfried von Strassburg praises him as a
living author in his *Tristan* (about 1210). But Heinrich von
dem Türlin, in his poem *Die Krone*, written between 1215 and
1220, refers to him as already dead.

Hartmann is looked upon as the founder of the court epic
— the creator of the classic poetic form of medieval German
literature, into which he was the first poet to introduce Arthurian legend. Charm, grace and moderation are the characteristics of his works. As Gottfried von Strassburg exclaims of
him in his *Tristan*, "How pure and how clear are his crystal-
line words!" Among his contemporaries, Hartmann's second
Arthurian epic, *Iwein*, was considered his masterpiece. In
form, it is the best Arthurian epic in German literature. We
of today, on the other hand, largely because its content is less
foreign to our world of thought, incline to give first place
among his works to *Der arme Heinrich*.

The poet's thoroughgoing change from the worldly material
of the Arthurian epic to the religious legend and then back
again is a remarkable one. It doubtless reflects the cross-
currents of his soul, which embraced a whole world of conflicting moods. The opposition between secular and religious
forces, which moved this whole age, left its mark upon Hartmann's life and works. He never overcame the conflict in his
nature between the wordly and the religious elements, nor was
he able to weld these elements harmoniously in his writings.
There came a time when his worldly epic grew to seem sinful
to him, and to call for literary penance. In the introduction
of his *Gregorius* he renounces everything earthly. In it he
expresses the idea that penitence and humility before God

purify and finally lift up even him who is laden with the most grievous sin. In *Der arme Heinrich* he teaches that without humility before God even the most excellent person cannot gain salvation. Each of these poems seeks to evaluate worldly pleasure as against devotion to God. After the writing of these two religious poems, Hartmann turns back once more in his *Iwein* to *Frau Welt*. In this narrative, as in his earlier *Erec*, he deals with the conflict between love and the duty of heroic knighthood. All four of his epics have an ethical basis, the moral action revolving about the two poles, guilt and atonement. The hero deviates from the order set for him, thus incurring guilt. But native goodness of character brings him through the test that works his restoration.

*Erec, Iwein* and *Gregorius* are free renditions of French poems into Middle High German. *Der arme Heinrich* is in a far higher degree an independent creation. In a general way, to be sure, its material belongs to world literature, as does that of *Gregorius*. The latter, a story of double incest, traces its pedigree from the Oedipus legend, while the former bears relationship to widespread stories of cleansing from leprosy through divine miracle or through human blood. If, with Hartmann, we identify Job's affliction as leprosy, the oldest work of literature in which the hero is a leper is the Book of Job. In German literature, the leper legend is found in the tale of *Sylvester*, the Latin *Amicus et Amelius*, Konrad von Würzburg's *Engelhard*, Kistener's *Jakobsbrüdern, Der Seelen Trost* and a story in *Die sieben weisen Meister*. And Crescentia too, in the *Kaiserchronik*, is afflicted with leprosy as a punishment.[50]

Hartmann gives his story a definite historical setting. He tells us in his prologue that he wishes to publish a tale which he found in a book, and that it is a story concerning a certain Herr Heinrich von Ouwe, a member of the noble family to which the poet rendered court service. From this it would seem that he was giving poetic treatment to a legend from the family annals of his lord. But a consideration arises to vex us.

---

[50] For references, consult Ehrismann, *Geschichte der deutschen Literatur,* p. 198.

How came he to learn from a book a tale with which, if it was a legend of his master's family, he should have been familiar from oral tradition? It would be possible to take the poet's citation of a source as an invention, a stylistic device to heighten interest by the weight of authority; yet the account seems too circumstantial. It seems more natural to assume that Hartmann did, in fact, read extensively, as he says, in search of edifying and consolatory material which he might use. He probably came upon some short Latin piece in a collection of legends or miracles; such stories, written for moralizing, instructional and devotional purposes, were common in the middle ages. Used often as sermon themes, these were called *exempla* or sermon stories. A short Latin version of *Der arme Heinrich* has in fact been found, in two Breslau collections of *exempla*. These date from the fourteenth and fifteenth centuries, but are based on older collections, of the thirteenth century. The story is on a low plane, calculated for the average public of a Sunday sermon. The two versions differ but little. A virgin is moved to sacrifice herself to cure a leper, because of gifts of clothes she had once received from him. The peasant family is lacking. In version A the leper is an Albertus, in B a Henricus. Passages which this Latin *exemplum* has in common with the book of Job, and which cannot have been taken from Hartmann's poem, seem to indicate that it does not originate from the latter, but antedates it.[50a] The poet probably read this or some similar short story and used the scant material as the basis of his poem. Just what lies at the bottom of his attaching the story to an ancestor of his noble master's family we do not know. Most probably he desired in this way to do honor to the family of his liege lord. But whatever scrap of narrative may have stimulated Hartmann to the use of his theme, he developed it into a moving story of his own, full of soul and religious warmth.[51]

The subject of the poem is almost repulsive, but as Uhland

---

[50a] Recent research by C. von Krause, "Drei Märlein . . . und das Exempel vom Armen Heinrich," 1930, casts grave doubt upon this view. Von Krause seeks to reverse the sequence, arguing that the *exemplum* is derived from Hartmann's A. H., and that Hartmann's source remains still to be discovered.

[51] *Ibid.*, p. 200.

remarks, "the mildest and most sincere of the old German poets has through his treatment poured out over the harshness of the old legend so soft and subdued a light that this poem stands out as one of the most excellent and graceful of the middle ages." Goethe, although he appreciated the high literary quality of the poem, felt himself strongly repelled by it. He writes:

The poem, which is in itself very admirable, gave me physical and aesthetic pain. One cannot help being nauseated by a leprous knight for whom a fine young girl sacrifices herself; as indeed a century in which the most repulsive disease has to serve so persistently as a motive for deeds of love and chivalry inevitably fills us with aversion. Upon me at least, that terrible disease as a motive for an act of heroism has an effect so violent that it seems to me the mere touching of the book exposes me to contagion.[52]

But those who are familiar with the fondness of medieval legend for the hideous and terrible, and who recall how even a poet such as Konrad von Würzburg, intimate with the refinement of court poetry, does not hesitate in one of his narratives to describe in loathsome detail the leprosy from which his hero suffers, will be less inclined to join in Goethe's criticism than to pay tribute to Hartmann's fine sensibility. He does not with a single word conjure up the horrid manifestations of Heinrich's affliction; he is content to show its blighting and tragic effect upon the hero's life, bringing out the sharp contrast between his state of friendless desertion and his former brilliant station. Soon the interest is occupied by the maiden, in whom the ethical content of the poem centers. She is pictured as a young saint. She has no inner battles to fight, no stirrings of earthly instincts to suppress, no clinging to life to overcome. Her native, self-sacrificing goodness of heart is strengthened by a mystic longing for heaven. In a state of sustained transport she presses firmly toward her goal of self-sacrifice for another. To be sure, the pious speeches of the young child to her parents impress us as all too wise, her attitude toward the torture she faces as all too light-hearted; and yet, bearing in

---

[52] *Tag- und Jahreshefte,* 1811, pp. 72 f.

mind that hers is the wisdom of poverty, and her psychology that of incipient puberty, we feel that she has not been drawn so untrue to life as some critics are inclined to believe. Moreover, Hartmann furnishes motivation in the atmosphere of wonder and miracle which surrounds the maiden. The Holy Ghost has inspired her with wisdom and eloquence and has prompted her to her task. Nor is such a spirit of transport foreign to the times. We have but to recall the religious frenzy which gripped young and old alike, and found expression in the children's crusades and in deeds of grimmest asceticism, to realize that we have here a breath of the middle ages.

A pleasing feature of Hartmann's narrative is that, while in most similar legends the bloody sacrifice is completed and must then be undone by a miracle, the sacrifice is here dispensed with, the will alone suffices.[53] The solution is entirely psychological. In Heinrich we trace a definite character development. Possessing wealth, high station and happiness, he lacks one virtue, the virtue of pious humility: he attributes his blessings to his own merit rather than to the grace of God. His guilt is due to his pride, *der hôhe muot*, the moral motivation of the action. Punished by God with leprosy, he passes into a state of misery out of which he works upward through stages of moral test. His first reaction is rebellion: he cannot find Job's patience to endure. But when all hope of a cure has vanished, his inner conversion begins. He proceeds from his pride to humility by three acts of piety: (1) he gives away his fortune; (2) he recognizes the guilt of his pride; (3) he purifies himself of his former worldliness by complete renunciation of cure and happiness and by humble surrender to God's will. Standing before the door of the doctor's room and perceiving the body of the girl lying prepared for the sacrifice, his inner conversion takes place (*er gewan einen niuwen muot*), his selfishness is changed to a new goodness (*in eine niuwe güete*). He has become ripe for God's mercy. The miraculous inspiration of the little maid to self-sacrifice and her moral strength

---

[53] In the *Sanct Sylvester* legend, too, the children in whose blood Emperor Constantine was to bathe are spared. Wackernagel-Stadler, *Der arme Heinrich*, pp. 171-177.

accomplish the healing of her master's soul, for her loyal devotion produces loyal devotion also in him, and works the miracle of his bodily cleansing. Both have withstood the test, for the fate that had been laid upon them was a test of God.

With all its atmosphere of miracle, of religious ecstasy and remoteness from earth, *Der arme Heinrich* affords us a realistic reflection of medieval life, with its social organization and its daily needs. The story is given a decided historical and local coloring. The impression of reality is heightened by the giving of the name and the home of the hero as with historical fidelity, and by the fact that this hero was an ancestor in the noble family which the poet himself served. We are led into an actual region in which Hartmann lived. Aside from the miraculous cure, almost everything could have happened as it is related: thoroughly realistic are the picture of the social classes; the plague of leprosy which was so rampant in medieval Europe, with the isolation of the stricken; the visiting of the most famous medical schools; life upon the rented farm; the loyalty of the peasant to his *seigneur*; the idyll of the child; the daughter's outlook upon her peasant life; the knightly equipment for the trip; the reception upon the return home; the praise of the native Swabians; and the summoning of kin and followers (*Magen und Mannen*) in conference over the marriage question. It is this strong realistic and historical trend blended with the legendary strain which makes the narrative so effective, and which so captures the interest of the present-day reader. The great number of text editions, of translations into modern verse and prose, and of dramatic re-castings which are listed in the Bibliography afford an eloquent testimony to the widespread interest in the poem, a translation of which is presented herewith for the first time in English verse.[53a]

Different in nature and content as are the two narrative poems which have been discussed above, they are alike in this, that each presents a peasant as an ideal figure. Hartmann von

---

[53a] A prior attempt, published in 1869 in an obscure place (*The Missouri Republican* [daily]), appears to have remained a fragment. See Bibliography, *The Golden Legend of Poor Henry*, by Kroeger.

Aue gives no personal names to the members of the peasant family which he pictures, not even to the daughter who plays so essential a rôle in the narrative. His peasant is an ideal type taken from a "sermon story," a pattern of Christian uprightness, and bearing an unlimited loyalty and devotion to his *seigneur* — a devotion which does not falter at housing and caring for the master stricken with leprosy when all the world forsakes and flees him, nor even at consenting to the sacrifice of his daughter for the cleansing of Herr Heinrich from his terrible disease.

Herr Heinrich's peasant is a freeman (*vrîer lantsaeze*), belonging to the third and lowest class of freeman as described by the law.[54] *Vollfrei* he is not, as he does not himself own the land which he tills. The farm or clearing which he cultivates is extensive, with small farmers or serfs resident on it, who are attached to the land. This holding, together with its bondsmen, is the personal inherited property of Herr Heinrich. The peasant is not a *Meier* in the original sense of this term: he has no managerial duties toward Heinrich — that is, he does not act as superintendent and collector of peasant rentals — but rents or leases the land from Heinrich in his own right. His favorable position is emphasized:[55] the landlord is content with his tenant and does not demand of him more than the latter of his own volition gives, either in regular rentals or in special levies. We are told also that Herr Heinrich protects his *Meier* from any outside violence or oppression,[56] a protection which he is under no obligation to afford his tenant.[57] Of other peasants it is explicitly stated that they had worse landlords.

Herr Heinrich, when he learned the hopelessness of a cure for his disease, gave away all his personal property to the Church and to his poor relatives, reserving for himself only the one farm to which he repaired. On the other hand, his rights of fief which belonged to his house he did not lose, despite his leprosy.[58] These rights left him the wherewithal to

---

[54] *Sachsenspiegel*, ch. 2.      [55] Vss. 267 ff.      [56] Vss. 270 ff., 278 ff.
[57] Cf. Schönbach, *Über Hartmann von Aue*, p. 309.
[58] Cf. *Sachsenspiegel*, I, 4.

pay for his keep and to undertake his second journey to Salerno. They are also the source of his increased wealth mentioned toward the end of the poem,[59] when, out of gratitude for his cure through the daughter, Heinrich presents the farm, together with the serfs upon it, as a gift to his faithful *Meier*, who thus becomes a landed peasant, a *Vollfreier*. The close of the narrative witnesses a marriage alliance between nobleman and peasant, for Herr Heinrich marries the freeman's daughter.

The poem *Meier Helmbrecht*, some fifty years later in date, pictures to us a peasant in a somewhat different position, and supplies a vastly greater amount of realistic detail. In this family grandfather, father and son were each named Helmbrecht. It appears that the father Helmbrecht was a freeman. He rents or leases his farm of medium size, possibly from some nobleman, more probably from a neighboring monastery. The lease had been held by his father before him,[60] and it is his ardent desire to hand it down to his son.[61] He tells us that he pays annually a tenth of his produce, and later states that he gives nothing to the monks other than their legal tithe.[62]

Besides the father and the mother, the Helmbrecht family consists of the son Helmbrecht and two daughters, Gotelint[63] and an older married sister who had left home after her marriage.[64] The father does not seem to have many hired helpers. He and his son do their own plowing, and the women of the family are accustomed to hard work, such as flailing grain, swinging and beating flax, digging up beets[65] and looking for the calves grazing in the brush.[66] Of servant helpers only two are mentioned, a man and a woman servant ( *der kneht* and *das friwip*).[67] These are free laborers, and not serfs bound to

---

[59] Vss. 1430 ff.      [60] Vs. 914.      [61] Vss. 543 ff.

[62] The cheeses and eggs taken to court by the Helmbrechts (vss. 913 ff.) have been interpreted as a form of rental payment. But the statement in vs. 918 that this was a common peasant practice makes it appear likely that it was merely a marketing of produce.      [63] Vs. 117.

[64] Vs. 1416. Haertel, "Social Conditions in Southern Bavaria," *loc. cit.*, p. 1059, overlooks the married daughter. He seems to interpret wrongly too the ironical utterance of the son Helmbrecht in vs. 364, upon which he bases an inference that there were several sons.

[65] Vs. 1359.      [66] Vs. 1391.      [67] Vss. 708, 711.

the soil as are the cottagers whom Herr Heinrich presents, together with the farm, to his tenant farmer.

Meier Helmbrecht possesses a fair amount of live stock. Horses are scarce. The son alludes to horse-raising;[68] but the father, to supply a suitable mount for his son, purchases one at a cost of thirty folds of woolen homespun, four cows, a yoke of oxen, three steers and four measures of grain.[69] Four other oxen are mentioned by name,[70] and reference is made to the calves out at pasture.[71] The mother raises poultry;[72] she and the daughter are able to present rich gifts, such as a cow, cheeses and eggs,[73] to the nun who made Helmbrecht's hood, and to dress the pampered youth like a young nobleman. The neighboring Meier Ruprecht offers his daughter's hand to young Helmbrecht with a dowry of ten cattle and many sheep and hogs,[74] an offer which he scorns: farming is altogether too slow with its returns, and he will have none of it.

Yet it is not for these details that we remember the father, Peasant Helmbrecht, and feel gratitude to Wernher for the rift which he makes in the mist that almost entirely hides the life of the common man of his time: it is rather for the rugged, steadfast, simple character which this old tiller of the soil reveals, for his integrity, and for his loyalty to his occupation. With what quiet manliness he talks of the dignity of labor! Agriculture has never been more heartily praised than by the elder Helmbrecht, who would give his all to keep his son on the farm. To the latter he offers moral worth, rather than descent, as the talisman by which to test true nobility:

> My son, if you would noble be,
> I counsel you most faithfully,
> Be noble, then, in what you do!
> Good conduct, this is always true,
> Is crown of all true nobleness,
>
> Vss. 503 ff.

the same fine sentiment that is expressed by a great poet of our own tongue:

---

[68] Vs. 377.    [69] Vss. 390 ff.    [70] Vss. 815 ff.    [71] Vs. 1391.    [72] Vs. 223.
[73] Vss. 119, 126.    [74] Vss. 280 ff.

*From "Schaffende Arbeit und bildende Kunst im Altertum und Mittelalter," by Paul Brandt, by permission of Alfred Kröner Verlag.*

## A Twelfth-Century "Farmer's Almanac"

*Calendarium* from an illustrated copy of the Chronicle of Zweifalten.

Loke, who that is most vertuous alway,
Privee and apert, and most entendeth ay
To do the gentil dedes that he can,
And taak him for the grettest gentil man.[75]

The work of the farmer, the father Helmbrecht urges,
benefits alike the poor and the rich. Many a lady is by it
endowed with beauty, many a king crowned through its yield.
Indeed even the birds and the beasts, the eagle and the wolf,
all animate nature, profit from the labors of the farmer. Without him, he reflects, the world's pride would be a very small
thing, and working faithfully night and day in the field of duty
which life has allotted to one not only best serves one's fellow-
man, but best honors God. Among all the wavering characters
of the poem, he alone remains firmly planted as a staunch old
oak, even when the lightning blasts of fate blight him in the
dishonor and destruction of his son and daughter. His sentiments are strangely modern for the time in which he lived. In
reading them we feel that those dimly viewed generations are
remote only in time; that over the intervening chasm of years
they were inspired by ideals far less alien to us than we commonly suppose.

[75] Chaucer's *Tale of the Wyf of Bathe*, Oxford Chaucer, D, 1113-1116.

# MEIER HELMBRECHT

Guot zuht ist sicherlîche
Ein krône ob aller edelkeit.
— *Meier Helmbrecht*

# MEIER HELMBRECHT [1]

One writes of what to him occurred;
One tells what he has seen; a third
Of love alone sings his refrain,
While still a fourth one writes of gain;
5  A fifth one praises riches — gold;
A sixth lauds courage, high and bold.
Here I shall tell what happened me —
That is, what my own eyes did see. [2]
I saw, and this is true, I swear,
10  A peasant's son — a lad whose hair
Was curly and light blond as well.
His locks, which richly downward fell
Beyond his shoulders on each side,
Above within a hood were tied.
15  This hood was richly worked. I ween
That no one ever yet has seen
So many birds on hood arrayed;
Both doves and parrots were displayed
In neat embroidery on the hood.
20  Hear more at length what thereon stood.

A peasant — Helmbrecht was his name —
Was father to a youth — the same
Concerning whom this tale is spun;
Like father, so was named the son,
25  For Helmbrecht was the name of each.
In simple, short and homely speech
I now shall tell you what was found —
What wondrous things were sewed around —
Upon his hood or cap so neat. [3]
30  (My tale shall be without deceit —

I'm telling not from mere surmise.)
Behind, one saw a seam-band rise;
From back to front the edging led,
Across the middle of his head.
35 This band was worked with birds, all made
As though just flown from out the shade
Of neighboring Spessart's [4] woody lair.
Upon a peasant's shock of hair
Sat never better hood before
40 Than on his head young Helmbrecht wore.
This bumpkin, you must further hear,
Had on the side, toward his right ear,
All sewed upon this selfsame hood
(Shall I now say what thereon stood?)
45 A picture of the siege of Troy,[5]
When daring Paris for his joy
Stole the king of Greece's wife;
He loved her dearer than his life.
One saw there too how Troy was won,
50 And how Aeneas, fleet, did run,
Escaping thence, by ship to sea;
And how the towers fell finally,
As well as many walls of stone.
Alas that any peasant's son
55 Should ever wear a hood of such
A kind as makes one tell so much!

Hear from me further, if you would,
What elsewhere on this headpiece stood,
Filled out in silk. You may believe,
60 The tale in no wise does deceive.
Upon the left side of the hood
King Charlemagne [6] and Roland stood,
Turpin, with Oliver at hand —
A staunch and battling warrior band.
65 The wonders that their power and might
Wrought with the heathen were in sight:
Provence, as well as distant Arles,[7]
Were overcome by good King Karl;

With wisdom and with virile hands
70 He conquered all the Spanish lands,
Whose people heathen were before.
And would you hear how furthermore
(This is the truth, like all the rest)
The hood between its bands was dressed
75 Behind the head from ear to ear?
One saw the sons of Helche[8] here,
Who, struggling valiantly and well,
In battle by Ravenna fell
When Wittich grimly struck them down —
80 That wanton blade of ill renown —
Them and young Diether, too, of Bern.
And you may further wish to learn
What else this fop, this foolish lad,
Embroidered on his headpiece had.
85 This fool of God, this silly lout,
Had on the front, all round about,
Extending from his right ear round
To where his other ear was found
(I know from fact that this is right;
90 Now hear the rest about this sight!)
A border, wondrous to behold,
Of ladies gay, knights brave and bold;
Nor had there been forgotten there
A group of lads and lasses fair.
95 These all were in a dancing scene,
And worked with silk of softest sheen.
Between the ladies, two and two,
Just as they still in dancing do,
A knight stood holding each fair hand.
100 And over at the other end,
Between each pair of lasses went
A lad, hands clasped in merriment.
And fiddlers, too, were standing near.

It now remains that you should hear
105 How such a hood young Helmbrecht had,

This foolish, wild, and wanton lad.
As yet you have not heard me say
Whence had come the hood so gay.
The needle of a pretty nun
110 Embroidered it; and she had run,
Turned by her beauty, from her cell.
It happened to her, truth to tell,
As to her kind quite frequently
(Such ones my eyes so often see!)
115 Who, by their lower half misled,
Stand at last with shame-bowed head.
Now Gotlint, Helmbrecht's sister, won
The favor of this pretty nun
By giving her a fine fat cow.
120 Skilled with her hands, the latter now
Repaid them, as so well she could:
Made Helmbrecht both a suit and hood.
When Gotlint gave the cow to her,
Hear what further did occur:
125 The mother gave, the nun to please,
So many eggs and so much cheese,
The while in convent halls she ate
She ne'er had been thus satiate
With foods — so many eggs to crack,
130 And such fine cheeses without lack.
The sister gave her brother more,
To honor him, than's told before:
A linen shirt,⁹ of such fine weave
One scarce a better could receive.
135 The linen was so finely spun
That seven weavers each had run
Away before the eighth man's skill
The final weaving did fulfill.
Suit-cloth the mother gave him then,
140 So wonderful a specimen
That never had a tailor's shears
Cut out such goods in many years.
Inside with fleece the cloth was lined,

With skin of beast of such a kind
145 As grazes on the grassy field,
The whitest that the land could yield.
The mother also gave her son
A sword, a very handsome one,
And doublet made of links of chain.
150 For Helmbrecht nothing was too vain.
His every wish she tried to meet
And gave, his outfit to complete,
A dagger and a pouch. Behold,
These decked a youth both wild and bold!

155 Now when she thus had dressed her son,
He said: "Dear mother, I need one
Thing more to wear: it is a coat.
If I should be without it, note
How damaged and disgraced I'd be.
160 It should be made so handsomely
That when you see me in the same
Your heart within you will exclaim
That you are honored in your son,
No matter where his path may run."
165 Still laid away in folds she had
A handsome dress; it was too bad
She had to part with it the while,
To clothe her son in proper style.
She bought him cloth of blue, so fair,
170 Not here, indeed, nor anywhere
Had any peasant theretofore
Possessed a coat worth two eggs more
Than Helmbrecht's. What I say to you
Is by my word of faith quite true!

175 Now he could teach him virtue's ways,
And also how to gain high praise,
Who had advised him such a coat.
Upon its back the eye could note
From belt to neck in straight array
180 How button close to button lay.

These brightly gleamed like reddest gold.
And if you further would be told
Details about this coat, I'll try
To meet your wish and amplify.
185   Down from the collar, 'neath the chin,
A row of buttons did begin
That reached the girdle-buckles quite.
These buttons were of silver-white.
Such labor rarely one bestows
190   Upon one's coat or other clothes.
No peasant wore such costly work
Twixt Hohenstein and Haldenberk.[10]
And see now how this pleases you:
There were three crystal buttons, too,
195   And not too small, nor yet too big.
He held with these his coat so trig
Across his chest, the stupid lout.
The bosom was all round about
Bestrewn with buttons, fine and bright,
200   That cast afar their dazzling light:
Yellow, blue, green, black, brown, red
And white, to order as he'd said.
These gleamed with such a brilliant sheen
That at each dance where he was seen
205   Most loving glances on him fell,
From maidens and from wives as well.
They all were charmed his form to see.
Now I confess, quite honestly,
That while this youth was standing there
210   I'd win scant favor from the fair.
Where sleeve was on to bodice bound,
The seam which ran its edge around
Was spangled gay with many a bell;[11]
One heard their tinkle very well.
215   Whenever in the dance he sprang
He charmed the girls with their cling-clang.
Sir Neidhart,[12] if he still did live,
Him God would ample talent give;

42

NEIDHART VON REUENTHAL AND HIS PEASANTS
From a miniature of the Mannessische Liederhandschrift.

In better verse this he could tell
220 Than I can, that I know quite well!
Ere Helmbrecht's mother had bought his clothes,
His leather leggins and his hose,
Many a hen and egg was gone.

When at last the proud young son
225 Was thus decked out in gorgeous show,
"My will impels me forth to go,"
He said. "Dear father, your support
I need, that I may go to court.
My mother gifts has given me,
230 My sister too, so generously,
That, as I live! to my last day
I'll bear them in my heart alway."

This gave the father great unrest.
His son in irony he addressed:
235 "To match your clothes, I'll give a steed,
And one that runs with swiftest speed,
One that can take a hedge or pit —
At court you will have need of it —
One that can run the longest course.
240 How gladly I shall buy the horse
If one is cheaply to be had!
Meanwhile I beg, belovèd lad,
Give up the trip you plan to court!
The courtier's life is of a sort
245 Too hard for those, and not well fit,
Who have not always followed it.
Dear son, you drive the steer for me,
Or take the plow while I drive. We
Shall thus get all our acres plowed.
250 And you will near your grave and shroud
With fullest honor, as I do
(I flatter me that this is true),
For I've been upright, faithful, just,
And never have betrayed a trust;
255 What's more, I pay in full each year

My proper tenth[13] without arrear.
And thus far I have lived my life
Free from envy, free from strife."

Said he: "Dear father mine, I pray
260 You drop this subject right away!
It cannot now be otherwise.
I'm bound to see, with my own eyes
What knightly life is like! And know
That now no longer I shall go,
265 Your sacks a-riding on my neck.
Nor shall I longer at your beck
Shovel dung upon your cart.
God's damnation blight my heart
If I should drive your steers once more,
270 Or sow your oat-seed as before.
It ill becomes my dashing air,
Nor is it suited to my hair,
My flowing, blond and curly tress,
My well-conditioned, handsome dress,
275 My new-made coat, my hood so gay,
Its hawks and pigeons on display,
Embroidered by a lady's hand.
I'll never help you plow your land!"

"Stay here, dear son, and do not go!
280 For Peasant Ruprecht, as I know,
Will give to you his daughter's hand;
Ten cattle, too, I understand,
And swine and sheep, both young and old.
At court you'll hungry be, and cold.
285 Your bed will often be most hard,
You'll win no favor nor regard.
Now follow my admonishment,
'Twill bring you honor and content;
For seldom does it come to pass
290 That one can rise above one's class.
Your station is behind the plow.
You'll find, too, courtiers enow

44

Wherever you direct your pace.
You'll bring upon you but disgrace,
295    I swear it, son. If you must test
The truth of this, you'll be the jest
Of all born courtiers, as you'll see.
Control yourself, and follow me!"

"Father, once I have a steed
300    You will find that I can lead
Court-life with just as fine an air
As those who've always lived right there.
Whoever once my headpiece sees
With all its silk embroideries
305    Will take his oath upon first sight
That I who wear it am a knight,
Although I've driven many a cow,
Marked many a furrow with the plow.
Once I'm dressed so smart and fine
310    In all these handsome clothes of mine
That sister gave me yesterday,
And mother, too, in such array,
I tell you most assuredly,
Unlike my former self I'll be;
315    What though so many times before
I've threshed upon the threshing floor
And with the flail have laid around,
Or driven stakes into the ground.
Once I've clad both foot and limb
320    And made them look so neat and trim
In hose and Cordovan-made[14] shoes,
No one can tell, e'en though he choose —
No one will think then to allege —
That I have ever built a hedge.
325    If you will give to me the mount,
Peasant Ruprecht need not count
On me to take his girl to wife.
No petticoat shall rule my life!"

He said: "A moment silent stay

45

330 And hear, son, what I've got to say.
  Who follows good admonishment
  Gains from it honor and content.
  The child who both in word and deed
  His father's counsel will not heed
335 Will reap at last but harm; his name
  Will soon be overwhelmed with shame.
  Now if you simply will not hear,
  But class yourself as friend and peer
  Of courtier noble-born and high,
340 You'll meet with failure when you try.
  For this he'll only bear you hate.
  You should believe what I now state,
  That never will a peasant grieve
  At any harm you may receive.
345 And if a knight, a genuine one,
  Took all a peasant e'er had won,
  He'd fare much better, son, than you.
  You know how certainly that's true.
  For if *you* steal a peasant's food,
350 Dear son of mine, beloved and good,
  If once he gets you in his hand,
  You're pledge and hostage, understand,
  For all who've robbed of him before.
  On you he'll settle each old score.
355 Your pleas will fruitlessly be spent.
  He'll count himself God's instrument
  If he should slay you at your deed.
  My own dear son, believe and heed
  All that I say. Avoid all strife,
360 Stay here, and choose yourself a wife."

  "Whatever, father, be my fate,
  I'll not yield now, it's far too late!
  Forth I must fare upon the stage.
  Now others as your sons engage,
365 And let them sweat behind your plow.
  The cattle such as I drive now

Must bellowing before me flee.
I'd not be here for you to see
Except for lack of nag or steed.
370   That I can't ride at whizzing speed
Along with others, all on edge,
Go raiding through each peasant's hedge,
And drag him out by head of hair,
That gives me deep regret, I swear!
375   I'll not endure the pinch of need;
If in three years I should indeed
Raise one poor colt, one cow as well,
Such gain would be a bagatelle.
I'll go a-robbing every day,
380   That I may gain sufficient prey,
And ample victuals, free of cost;
And that my body from the frost
In winter's kept; unless it be
None buys my captured steers from me.
385   Father, hasten now straightway,
Do not make the least delay!
Give to me at once the steed
And let me swiftly from you speed!"

I will not let the story lag.
390   Some thirty yards of woolen shag
(And, as the tale would have us know,
This cloth of thirty folds[15] or so
Was longest of all lengths of shag),
He sold, to buy his son the nag;
395   Four finest cows, too, it appears,
A yoke of oxen and three steers,
Four measures also of his grain.
Alas, lost goods for all his pain!
For full ten pounds[16] he bought the horse,
400   And in that selfsame hour, of course,
At three it would have scarce resold;
The seven pounds were but lost gold.

When now the son thus ready stood,

Had donned his handsome clothes and hood,
405 Hear what the foolish youth then said.
He proudly shook his hooded head,
And in a vaunting, boastful tone
Said: "I could bite through hardest stone!
I feel such bold and valiant mood,
410 Heigh! I could chew up iron for food!
Let the Kaiser[17] count it gain
If I don't capture and enchain
And pluck him to the very hide;
Our good and noble duke beside,
415 Perhaps a count or two as well.
Cross fields I shall ride pell-mell
My course without the slightest fear,
Crisscross the world both far and near.
Now let me pass from out your care
420 To hurtle swiftly through the air.
In my own fashion I will grow.
A Saxon,[18] father, you must know,
You'd rear with greater ease than me!"

He said: "You may then, son, be free.
425 With your training I am through.
Henceforth I wash my hands of you!
My further counsel I must spare
As to the way you curl your hair.
However, guard your handsome hood
430 With all its doves, lest someone rude
Should touch it without gentleness,
And, with bad intent, might mess
Your long and light-blond locks thereby.
But if you really want to try
435 Without my guidance and my aid
To get along, I'm sore afraid
A staff will be your guide some day,[19]
Some child will lead you on your way."
He said: "O son, beloved young man,
440 Let me dissuade you from your plan!

48

Live here on what I live on too,
And on what mother gives to you.
Drink water, dearest son of mine,
Ere you with booty buy your wine.
445 Our meal-cake, even in Austria, son,
Is much enjoyed by everyone.
Both wise and stupid relish it —
For noblemen they deem it fit.
Do you, dear child, eat of it too,
450 Before you go so far that you
Exchange your stolen oxen when
You're hungry, for a paltry hen.
Each week day mother here can make
The best of soups, and no mistake!
455 Fill up your maw with that! 'Twill aid
You better than to give in trade
For someone's goose your stolen horse.
If you will only take this course
You'll live in honor, son, like me,
460 No matter where you chance to be.
Son, mix a little bit of rye
Together with your oats, and try
To be content with this good dish
Before you eat of stolen fish.[20]
465 Follow me, and you are wise;
If not, betake you from my eyes!
Though you win wealth and honor too,
I shall not wish to share with you;
And if you win disgrace and pain,
470 Alone bear these, as well as gain."

"You drink your water, father mine,
And I shall quench my thirst with wine.
Enjoy your groats, if you so wish,
But I prefer a better dish
475 Of chicken, boiled deliciously;
It cannot be forbidden me.
And I shall eat, until I'm dead,

The finest, whitest wheaten bread.
The oats are proper food for you.
480 The Roman law says, and it's true:
A child will, in his early days
Take on his sponsor's virtuous ways.[21]
A noble knight once sponsored me,
And blessed may he ever be.
485 Through him I am of noble kind,
And have a proud and knightly mind!"

The father said: "Believe me, son,
Who far more pleases me, is one
That follows only proper ways,
490 Does right, and always constant stays.
Though he by birth be somewhat low,
He'll please the world much better so
Than one of royal line or birth,
Devoid of virtue or of worth.
495 A worthy man of low degree,
And a noble without honesty
Or morals, you must understand,
Should both these enter some strange land
Where no one knew them, you would see
500 They'd take the man of low degree
To be the noble of high birth,
Not him who chooses shame for worth.
My son, if you would noble be,
I counsel you most faithfully,
505 Be noble, then, in what you do!
Good conduct, this is always true,
Is crown of all true nobleness.
That I am right, you must confess."

The son said: "Father, that is true.
510 But then, my hood, my long hair too,
My handsome clothes, all seem to say:
You can't stay rooted here! Away!
So brilliantly my garments gleam,
More fitting for a dance they seem

515   Then harrowing or plowing earth."

"Alas that mother gave you birth!"
Exclaimed the father to the son.
"Because you leave the best undone
And do the worst! My handsome youth,
520   Reply to this, and speak the truth
If you have common sense and wit,
Which has the better life of it:
He, whom all berate and curse,
Whose actions make the whole world worse,
525   Who lives from other people's woe,
And works against God's favor so:
Which life now is the purer, son,
His, or again, the life of one
From whom the whole world profit draws,
530   Who does not seem aggrieved because
He struggles hard, both day and night,
For others' gain, to live aright —
To God doth proper honor show;
And who, wherever he may go
535   Finds favor both with God and man?
Dear son, now tell me if you can —
But speak the truth — which of these two
Is the more pleasing man to you?"

"Father mine, it is the man
540   Who harms no one, but rather can
Bring gain and pleasure to mankind;
His is the better life, I find."

"And you would be that very one
If you would follow me, dear son.
545   Stay here at home and help me plow
And you will help the world enow.
You'll profit then both rich and poor
By such good work, you may be sure.
The wolf, indeed, the eagle too,[22]
550   All creatures will rejoice for you,

All living things of sea and land
Called into life by God's command.
Belovèd son, stay by the plow,
For with its gain it can endow
555 With beauty many a dame. 'Tis found
That many a king himself is crowned
Through gains our farming-labors buy.
And no one ever stood so high
Whose pride would not endure a fall
560 If farming were not done at all."

"From your sermons, sire, I pray
God grant to me release straightway.
If by chance you had turned out
A genuine preacher, I don't doubt
565 But that your sermons would have made
A grand success with some crusade!
Now what I wish to say, please hear:
Though peasants do much work, I fear
They eat up more than is their share.
570 And now, however I may fare,
I certainly will plow no more!
If soiled and blackened hands I wore
Because I did the plowing here,
Then by the grace of God, it's clear
575 I should be shamed, beyond all chance,
When I took ladies' hands in dance."

The father said: "My son, demand —
And be not vexed at my command —
Wherever you may wise men see,
580 Just what this dream I dreamed might be:
You had two candles in your hand.
These burned, until far over land
Their rays shone clear, and brightly beamed.
The man of whom I last year dreamed,
585 Loved son, a dream of this same kind,
I saw him this year walking blind!"

The son said: "Father, very well!
But if perchance my courage fell
At such a tale, then certainly
590 An arrant coward I should be!"

This warning failed, like those before.
The father said: "And I dreamed more:
One foot you walked on, painfully;
Your other leg, off at the knee,
595 Was resting on a wooden crutch.
From out your coat there stuck some such
A thing as splintered shoulder blade!
That profit from this dream be made,
Ask what its hidden sense may be,
600 Of all the wise men that you see!"

"That means good luck, health free from care,
Of all rich joys a goodly share!"

He said: "A further dream I dreamed,
And shall I tell you how it seemed?
605 It seemed to me you wished to fly
O'er woods and brush, high in the sky.
Somehow, a wing was clipped off short.
This put an end to all your sport.
Does this dream, also, good foretell?
610 Alas, hands, feet, and eyes as well!"

"Father, all of these your dreams
Foretell my happiness, it seems,"
Said Peasant Helmbrecht's youthful son.
"For servant, seek some other one.
615 You'll now be left behind by me,
No matter what your dreams may be."

He said: "These dreams, compared with one,
Are but a puff of wind, my son!
Hear one dream more that came to me:
620 I saw you standing on a tree.
Above the grass your feet, I swear,

53

Were near two fathoms in the air.
Perched above your head so high
A raven sat, a crow near by.
625 Your hair was matted and unkempt.
These two birds combed it, as I dreamt:
From right the crow would dart at it,
From left the raven parted it.
Alas, this dream that I did see,
630 Alas, oh son, alas the tree!
Alas the raven and the crow!
I've ill succeeded, as I know,
In what I've brought you up to be,
Unless the dream has lied to me."

635 "By Christ! And father, though it seems
You've dreamed all that there is of dreams,
Both of the good and evil too,
I'll ne'er give up, whate'er I do,
The trip I long for, till my death.
640 I feel its need with every breath.
Dear father, may God care for you,
And care for dearest mother, too!
His kindness on your children rest,
And may they be forever blessed!
645 God keep us all within his care!"
With this, young Helmbrecht forth did fare;
To father his farewell once said,
Through the gate he quickly sped.
If I related *all* his ways,
650 Then not within three livelong days —
Perhaps, indeed, not in a week —
Could I make end and cease to speak.

He, riding on, reached castle walls.[23]
The knight who ruled within its halls
655 From warfare ample booty gained;
And so, most gladly he retained
Whoever did not fear to ride
And fight his foemen at his side.

54

The youth became a squire to him.
660 His plundering became so grim,
What others scarcely would attack
He thrust within his greedy sack.
He pilfered anything at all;
No booty was for him too small,
665 Nor could it be too big for him.
It might be shaggy, sleek, or slim,
It might be straight, or have a crook —
All, just the same, our Helmbrecht took,
The peasant Helmbrecht's ill-starred son.
670 He'd take a horse from anyone,
Or cow, and scarce a spoonful leave.
Of sword and doublet he'd relieve
A man — of mantle and of coat.
He took his kid, he took his goat,
675 He took the sheep, the ram beside;
He paid it later with his hide!
He'd even take a woman's skirt,
From off her back he'd pull the shirt,
Her coat of skin, her cloak, or gown.
680 But when the sheriff tamed him down
He felt the deepest sort of rue
That he had robbed from women too;
The truth of this will soon appear.
Good fortune favored his first year;
685 Fine sailing-wind hummed overhead,
His craft in safety forward sped.
His daring then grew greater yet,
Because the best share he would get
Of captured booty and of prey.
690 But now his thoughts began to stray
Towards his own kin. All those that roam
Thus feel themselves at times drawn home.
So from his lord he took his leave;
His comrades likewise did receive
695 His farewell wishes, that God might
Keep them in his watchful sight.

Here comes a chapter to relate
Which it were hard to relegate
To silence, and forbear to tell.
700 If only I could picture well
How those at home received the youth!
Did they walk toward him? No, forsooth,
They did not walk, they ran instead.
All in a heap they sprang ahead.
705 Each one before the other pushed.
The father, mother, leapt and rushed
As though no calf of theirs had died.[24]
What did the servant who first spied
The lad receive for such good news?[25]
710 Shirts and breeches he well could use.
Did the hired folk[26] then straight out
"Welcome, Helmbrecht!" gaily shout?
That by no means did they do,
For well had they been charged not to!
715 But rather: "Sir," both spoke instead,
"God's welcome to you, sir!" He said:
*"Min leiwe säute Kindekin,*
*Gott lass euch immer selig sin!"* [27]
His sister ran up to him then.
720 She threw her arms around him; when
With these strange words he next addressed her,
As greeting to her: *"Gratia vester!"*
The young ones in the lead we find;
The parents panted on behind.
725 They showered their greetings on the lad.
*"Dieu vous salue!"* replied the cad
To father; and to mother so,
Bohemianwise: *"Dobré jitró!"*
Between these two a look was sent
730 That showed their great astonishment.
The wife spoke: "Husband, I believe
Our senses fool us and deceive!
He's not our child, but, I contend,
Bohemian, or else a Wend."

735 The father spoke: "A Frenchman he.
My son, whom I did faithfully
Commend to God, he's not, I swear,
Although he's like him to a hair."
Then Gotlint, sister of the youth,
740 Said: "He is not your son, in truth!
He spoke in Latin words to me;
He is a priest or monk, maybe."
"My faith!" declared the hired hand,
"If I correctly understand,
745 This youth was reared in Saxony,
Or Flanders, that is plain to see.
'Leiwe Kindekin,' said the youth;
He must be Saxon then, forsooth!"

Simply the father spoke, and slow:
750 "Son Helmbrecht, is it you, or no?
If my heart you wish to win
Speak but a word as all your kin
And kith at home have always done,
That I may know you are my son.
755 'Dieu vous salue!' you say, or so,
But what that means I do not know.
Honor me, and mother, too;
We both deserve as much from you.
Speak a single German word!
760 I'll rub your horse when that I've heard,
Myself, and not my hired hand —
A word that I can understand;
And blessings on you, son Helmbrecht."

"Wat hewwt ihr dummer Bur mi seggt,[28]
765 Und das vermoledete Wif?
Min Pird un minen smucken Lif
Sall mir ein plumper Buersmann
Wahrhaftig nimmer gripen an!"

This speech alarm in him awoke,
770 But still the father kindly spoke:

"If you're my son, my Helmbrecht, then
Tonight I'll boil for you a hen,
And also roast a second one.
I'll keep this promise to you, son.
775 But if you're *not* Helmbrecht, my child,
But foreign Wend, Bohemian wild,
Betake you to the Wends! God knows,
Trials enough I have, and woes,
In caring solely for my own.
780 And only barest dues alone
Shall priest or monk receive from me!
If you're *not* Helmbrecht, certainly,
Though I had amplest stores of fish,
You'd never get a single dish,
785 Nor at my table wash your hand.[29]
If you're from Saxony, Brabant,
Or if again you come from France,
It's well if in your bag perchance
You have provisions with you now;
790 For you will never then, I vow,
Touch food of mine, I'd have you hear,
Not though the night should prove a year!
No wine or mead is on my board.
Young sir, go stay with some rich lord!"

795 Now it was growing on toward night.
Young Helmbrecht counseled left and right
Within himself, and then said he:
"As true as God my help may be,
I'll tell you who I am, straight out!
800 For nowhere is there round about
A host who would receive me.
It was not sharp, believe me,
My speech to you thus to disguise.
I'll act no more in such a wise."
805 He said, "Yes, I am he, it's true!"

The father said, "Well, say then who!"
"The one who bears your selfsame name."

58

The father said: "Declare the same!"
"They call me Helmbrecht, after you.
810 Your son, and also servant, too,
I was, and but a year ago;
And this I swear to you is so."
"I think you lie," the father spoke.
" 'Tis true!" "Then name to me the yoke
815 Of oxen four in front of you!"
"That I can very quickly do.
That ox, that formerly I took
So oft in charge, and o'er it shook
My stick, we called it 'Heather.'
820 I'm very doubtful whether
There ever farmer was who would
Not own such cattle if he could.
And that next ox, we called him 'Spot.'
A prettier creature no one's got,
825 Or ever harnessed up in yoke!
The third, too, I can name," he spoke,
"We called that tricky creature 'Spite.'
It is because my mind's so bright
That all their names I still can tell.
830 And will you further prove me? Well,
The other ox's name is 'Sun.'
That I can name them, every one,
Let that to my advantage be,
And have the door unbarred for me!"
835 The father said: "At door and gate
Shall you no longer stand and wait;
And every chamber, every chest,
Shall open be at your request."

Misfortune, may you cursèd be!
840 For never has there come to me
Such goodly treatment, of a truth,
As now was given to the youth.
His horse out to the stall was led.
And for himself the finest bed

845 Did sister, mother, then prepare.
The father tended to the fare.
He furnished food with lavish hand.
Much as I've wandered through the land
Such kindly care I've nowhere had
850 As was bestowed upon this lad.
The mother to her girl did cry:
"Now do not walk, my child, but *fly*
Up to our storeroom in the loft
And bring down bolster and pillow soft."
855 These things upon the stove were spread
To make a warm, luxurious bed,[30]
That he might rest upon the same
Until the time for dinner came.
When Helmbrecht had awaked again
860 The dinner was prepared, and then
He washed his hands. I'll now relate
What food was placed before his plate.
I'll name the course they first set down
(Were I a man of high renown
865 I'd always most contented be
If this same dish were served to me):
As fine-cut kraut[31] as you will find;
And fat and lean (there was each kind)
Came with this dish — the best of meat.
870 Now hear what food he next did eat:
A soft and ripe and fatty cheese
Was served and cut, the youth to please.
A third dish followed then, to wit,
As fat a goose as e'er on spit
875 Was roasted at a kitchen fire.
(The parents did not seem to tire,
They did all this with best of will.)
This fowl had grown so large until
'Twas big as ever buzzard is,
880 And now the youth could call it his.
A boiled hen and a roasted one,
As Helmbrecht's father ordered done,

Were now brought on the groaning board.
Such food would surely please a lord;
885 He'd glad enough eat just the same
While in his blind he ambushed game.
Many other dishes, too,
The like a peasant never knew,
Foods fine and good as could be had,
890 Were now served up before the lad.
The father said: "If I had wine
We'd drink it now, dear son of mine.
Instead, loved Helmbrecht, take for drink
This fine spring water, best, I think,
895 That ever from the earth did flow.
No equally good spring I know
Except the Wanghaus[32] spring so clear;
But no one brings its waters here."

While thus they joyfully all ate,
900 The father could no longer wait;
He asked his son to tell the sort
Of life he had observed at court
Where he was present, while away.
"Tell what court-life is like today,
905 And I in turn will tell you then
How I, long years ago, and when
I still my youthful years enjoyed,
Observed how knights their time employed."

"You, father, tell that first to me,
910 And I shall then tell willingly
Whatever you may ask me to.
Of customs I know much that's new."

"When I was young, long years ago,
Your Grandpa Helmbrecht (as you know,
915 This is the name my father had)
Sent me to court, though but a lad,
With eggs, and with his cheeses too,
Just as a peasant still will do.

And many knights I saw those days,
920 Observed their customs and their ways.
Those knights were courtly, stately men,
And knew no knavish evil then
As in these times so many do —
So many men, and women, too!
925 One picturesque and knightly way
Won favor with the ladies gay:
'Tourney' is what they called the game.
A courtier gave to me its name
When I requested him to tell
930 About this sport they liked so well.
They rode as though their ire were raised
(Because of this I heard them praised).
One group rode here, the other there,
Against each other, pair and pair,
935 As though to thrust each from his horse.
Among my comrades I of course
Had never witnessed any sort
Of game like this I saw at court.
When they had finished with the lance
940 They trod the measures of a dance
Accompanied by dashing song.
To no one did the time seem long.
Forth stepped a fiddler then straightway
Who for the dance began to play.
945 The ladies then did all arise —
A sight to gladden moping eyes.
The knights stepped forth towards beauty's band
And clasped their partners by the hand.
There was an overflow of charm,
950 Fair ladies led on knighthood's arm —
A pretty feast for eyes to see;
And in the dance joined merrily
Young men and maidens, poor and rich,
It did not seem to matter which.
955 The dance then over, from the crowd
Someone stepped forth and read aloud

About Duke Ernest.[33] At the close,
Whatever each one present chose
For pleasure, that he found to do:
960 Some shot with bow and arrow, too,
Toward distant targets that were set.
And there were other pleasures yet:
Some hunted game, some chased the hind.
Who then was worst in every kind
965 Of skill, would be the best today.
Ah! In those days so far away
Good faith was prized, and honor too,
Ere falseness spoiled these through and through.
The false and loose and evil men
970 Who with their knavish cunning then
Knew how to make the wrong seem right
The knights did not permit in sight
To dine at court in honor's guise.
Today that one is counted wise
975 Who can deceive and lie; in short,
He is a valued man at court,
Wins honor and wins money too,
Far more (unhappily 'tis true)
Than does a man who lives upright,
980 And strives for favor in God's sight.
This much of older ways I know;
And now the favor to me show,
Loved son, and tell me of the new."

"In truth, and that I'll do for you.
985 This is the present knightly way:
'Drink, comrade, drink again, I say!
Drain you your goblet, I'll drain mine!
We'll be the better for the wine!'
Now listen: this is what I mean:
990 Of yore the worthy knights were seen
Where pretty ladies lingered round.
Today they're always to be found
Where wine is kept for sale. And there

This constitutes their only care,
995 As eve and morn they drinking sit:
How they can quickest see to it
(If once the kegs they empty drain)
That their good host new stores may gain
Of wine as stout and heady,
1000 To keep their spirits ready.
This is the minnesong they sing:
'Come, barmaid, pretty little thing,
Our cups must overflowing be!
A monkey and a fool were he
1005 Whose body ever should incline
To worship women more than wine!'
He who can lie has good address;
Deceiving — that is courtliness.
He counts as skilled whose edged tongue can
1010 Maliciously insult a man.
Who curses others like a knave
Is deemed both virtuous and brave.
Believe me, father, it is true,
Old-fashioned people such as you
1015 Are now all under social ban!
They are to woman and to man
About as welcome company
As is the hangman wont to be!
The ban itself is but a joke!"

1020 "A mercy God!" the father spoke,
"Be it lamented in our prayers
That wickedness so much now dares!"

"The former jousts are in disgrace,
And new ones occupy their place.
1025 Before, one heard them call out gay:
'Halloo, sir knight, on to the fray!'
But now they cry the whole day through:
'Pursue them, knight, chase and pursue!
Thrust and thrust, and slay and slay!
1030 Thrust out the eyes that see the day!

Strike off a foot there where it stands,
And here hew off a pair of hands!
Hang this fellow here for me,
Catch the rich men that you see —
1035  They'll yield a hundred pounds or so.'
These customs very well I know.
I trow I could, did I incline,
Relate much more, dear father mine,
That's new, about such ways. 'Twill keep!
1040  I've ridden far, and I must sleep.
Tonight I am in need of rest."
They did all things at his request.
Of sheets the household knew no trace.
A fresh-washed shirt, then, in its place,
1045  Which sister Gotelint had kept,
She spread upon his bed. He slept
Until the following morning late.
What he did then, I'll next narrate.

As one might very well expect,
1050  Young Helmbrecht now the table decked
With all the gifts of every sort
That he had brought along from court
For father, and mother, and sister too.
And of a truth, if you but knew
1055  What these consisted of, I'm quite
Convinced that you would laught outright.
His father he brought a whetting-stone —
No mower could a better own
To tie in handle with a band;
1060  A scythe, so fine that peasant's hand
Ne'er swung the like of it through hay —
A peasant's gem in every way!
A hatchet in his hand he laid,
And never had a better blade
1065  Or one so good been forged by smith.
He gave him, too, a hoe therewith.
Among these things, another

Was a fox-skin for his mother.
Helmbrecht, with a stunning whack
1070 Had stripped it from a fat priest's back.
What Helmbrecht stole or took as prey
I'll not conceal in any way,
Although I may not know the whole.
From a traveling mercer, too, he stole
1075 A very handsome silken band,
Which now he put in Gotlint's hand,
As well as gold-embroidered lace
That far more suitably would grace
Some noble's child who knew no stint,
1080 Than Helmbrecht's sister Gotelint.
The hired man Helmbrecht brought lace shoes;
But for him he ne'er would choose
To carry such coarse things along
Or even touch a dirty thong,
1085 He was so courtly. Had he staid
At home to be his father's aid,
He would have left him bare of foot.
In the hired maid's hand he put
A neckerchief and ribbon red,
1090 Two things that stood her in good stead.

How long, you now would have me say,
Did Helmbrecht with his father stay?
But seven days, it is the truth.
It seemed a whole year to the youth
1095 Since he had taken any prey.
So now he made all haste to say
Good-by to father, mother, both.
"No, no, dear son," the father quoth,
"If you but think that you can live
1100 With what I own and have to give
Until my efforts here are done,
Then sit, and wash your hands, dear son;
Go in and out as pleases you.
With court-life have no more to do.

*From "La Sculpture française," by J. Roussel,
Éditions Albert Morancé, by permission.*

## The Peasant
From the cathedral of Notre-Dame, Paris.

1105 'Twill bitter prove, as you will see.
       Much rather I'd a peasant be
       Than some retainer of a court
       Who no farm rental gets — in short,
       Who must for once and all prepare
1110 To forage for his daily fare,
       Must scurry round now there, now here,
       And constantly endure the fear
       That if his foes once capture him
       They'll hang him to the nearest limb."

1115 "Father," spoke the handsome lad,
       "For the welcome I have had,
       Sincere and cordial thanks of mine!
       But since the time I last drank wine
       A week or more's already passed.
1120 Because of this extended fast
       My belt is three holes smaller now.
       Beef I must have from toothsome cow
       Before my buckle goes once more
       Back to the place where it was before.
1125 I'll spoil the day of many a plow
       And take as booty many a cow
       Before I give my body rest
       To round out nicely to its best.
       There is a certain wealthy man
1130 Who's given me insult greater than
       Any one I've ever seen.
       Godfather's crops of tender green
       I saw him ride across of late.
       Now well he knew, if he'd but wait,
1135 His pay must be an ample one.
       His cattle very soon must run,
       His sheep, and also all his swine.
       That for this godsire loved of mine
       He trampled down his hard-earned grain,
1140 This makes me feel the deepest pain.
       I know another rich man who

Has offended deeply, too!
For with his crullers he ate bread! [34]
If I don't punish this, I'm dead!
1145 A third rich man is known to me,
And no one quite so much as he
Has hurt my feelings, I declare!
Not even would a bishop's prayer
Persuade me vengeance to forego,
1150 His conduct has offended so!"

His father asked him: "What is that?"
"While at his table still he sat
He opened wide his belt, the boor.
Heighho! for that, you may be sure
1155 All that's his I'll snatch away!
His beasts shall all be mine one day
That haul his cart and drag his plow.
They'll help me, so that I shall now
For Christmas have fine clothes to hand.
1160 How did he think that I would stand
Such insults? O the triple fool!
He, and another empty skull
Who's hurt my deepest feelings so?
If unavenged I let this go,
1165 Then let them call me slave of fear.
He, drinking from a mug his beer,
Blew from its top the gathered foam.
Did I not pay such insult home,
With ladies I should have no worth,
1170 And never more about my girth
Should I deserve to hang a sword.
And now full soon you shall have word
Of me and of the swath I'll cut.
Many a farmyard I shall gut,
1175 And if my man is gone that day,
I'll drive his stock off, anyway."

The father said: "I'll thankful be,
My son, if now you'll name to me

68

Your comrades all — the fellows who
1180 Have taught you it's the thing to do
To take revenge upon rich men
And confiscate their cattle when
With crullers they perhaps eat bread.
I'd like to hear their names," he said.

1185 "There's Lämmerslint,[35] a comrade fair,
And Schluckdenwidder; that's the pair
From whom I've learned to know the trade.
I'll name you other friends I've made:
There's Höllensack, and Rüttelschrein —
1190 These both were teachers, too, of mine.
There's Mausdenkelch, Kuhfrass as well.
Now, father, you have heard me tell
With what fine blades it is I mix;
Already I have named you six.
1195 Wolfsgaum's another comrade. He,
No matter what his love may be
For cousin, uncle, aunt — or whether
It be February weather —
Leaves no thread upon their form,
1200 Man or woman, to keep them warm,
Or even cover up their shame.
Strangers and kin he treats the same.
Wolfsrüssel, he's a man of skill!
Without a key he bursts at will
1205 The neatest-fastened iron box.[36]
Within one year I've seen the locks
Of safes, at least a hundred such,
Spring wide ajar without a touch
At his approach! I can't say how.
1210 Horse, ox, and also many a cow,
Far more than I can tell about,
From barn and farm he's driven out;
For when he'd merely toward it start,
Each lock would quickly spring apart.
1215 I've still one further comrade, sire.

And never did a knight's good squire
Win for himself such courtly name.
He had it from a wealthy dame,
A duchess of most high degree
1220 Who's known as Nonarre Narrie.[37]
This comrade's name is Wolfesdarm.
And whether it be cold or warm,
He cannot pillage to his fill.
For theft so gratifies his will,
1225 His thirst for it he cannot slake.
No footstep does he ever take
Away from evil toward the good;
With instinct sure his spirit would
Strive toward bad and vicious deed
1230 As does a crow to new-sown seed."

The father said: "Now I would learn
What name they have for you in turn,
Each one of all your comrades gay,
When there is something he would say."

1235 "Father mine, this is my name,
For which I feel no need of shame:
My comrades call me Schlingdasgeu.
I seldom bring the peasants joy
That in our neighborhood are found.
1240 Their children, where I've been around
Eat water-soup that's thin and flat.
I make them suffer more than that!
I quickly press the one's eyes out,
On others' backs I lay about,
1245 Across an ants' nest one I stake,
Another's beard I jerking take
With pincers piecemeal from his face,
Break this one's limbs in many a place,
Tear that one's scalp off while he squeals,
1250 String up by the tendons of his heels[38]
Another one, with withes for twine.
All that the peasants have is mine!

70

Where we ten comrades ride along,
What though our foe be twenty strong
1255 Or even more, and stalwart men,
They're soon laid low by our bold ten."

"My son, these comrades that you name,
Although it's true you know the same
Better than do I, my child —
1260 However bold they are, and wild,
If watchful God ordains it so,
The sheriff, as you well must know,
Can make them go where'er he will,[39]
And were they thrice his number still."

1265 "Father, what till now I've done,
Not for a king or anyone
Will I continue any more!
Geese and chickens by the score,
Your cattle, cheeses, and your hay
1270 For you and mother till today
I've saved from all my friends for you.
Now this I will no longer do;
For you've offended far too much
The honor of my comrades, such
1275 As no misdeeds have ever done
In robbing goods of anyone.
Had not you so complained and carped,
And on our evil doings harped,
To Lämmerslint, as I had planned,
1280 I should have given Gotlint's hand —
To Lämmerslint, my comrade good.
She'd had the finest livelihood
That any woman ever won
With husband since the world begun.
1285 Furs, mantles, best of linen too,
As fine as ever churchman knew,
Should have been hers in ample measure,
Had you not, in your displeasure
Slanders on us wished to speak.

1290   And Gotlint would have had each week,
      If she had wished, the freshest meat
      From newly slaughtered cow, to eat."

      "Sister Gotelint, now hear:[40]
      When Lämmerslint, my comrade dear,
1295   First sought to gain your hand through me
      I answered unreservedly:
      'As things with you and her now stand,
      Believe me, if you win her hand,
      This you will never have to rue.
1300   I know that Gotelint's so true
      (Of this you need not anxious be),
      That if you're hanged once on a tree,
      Herself she'll cut the rope in two,
      Will drag you off, and bury you
1305   Near by where crossing roads do meet;[41]
      With myrrh and burning incense sweet
      (You may be sure of this all right)
      She will encircle you each night
      For one whole year or thereabout;[42]
1310   And you may know beyond all doubt,
      She'll smoke your bones when none else would,
      Your bones which are so pure and good.
      But if by fortune you are left,
      And of your eyesight are bereft,
1315   She'll guide your footsteps through the land,
      Through paths and bypaths, with her hand.
      If you should lose a foot or two,
      The crutches which are used by you
      Each morning to your bed she'll bear.
1320   And you need also feel no care
      If, with the foot they cut from you,
      One hand or more is lopped off, too.
      As long as you still live to eat
      She'll cut for you your bread and meat.'

1325   "Lämmerslint then spoke. Said he:
      'If Gotelint says yes to me,

To her a dowry I shall give,
So that the better she may live.
Three well-filled sacks belong to me;
1330 They weigh like lead, these sacks, all three.
One's full of uncut cloth; she'll find
The finest linen of its kind.
If one should buy a yard in trade
Fifteen good *kreutzers* would be paid.
1335 This gift she certainly will prize.
The second sack will please her eyes
With veils, and skirts, and many a waist;
And poverty no more she'll taste
If we are man and wife. I swear
1340 I'll give her all these things to wear
Upon the very following day,
. And all I take henceforth as prey.
The third sack bulges to its brim,
Stuffed full, up to its very rim,
1345 With finest cloths and feathery fur.
And there will also be for her
Two mantles that are scarlet-lined;
An outside trimming she will find
Of sable fur, both soft and black.
1350 I've safely hidden each stuffed sack
In a ravine not far away.
I'll give her these without delay.'

"Your father's ruined all I'd planned.
May God protect you with his hand!
1355 You're like to lead a bitter life.
If any peasant as his wife
Should take you, you are very sure
The direst hardship to endure.
You'll flail his grain, your strength he'll tax,
1360 And you must swing and beat his flax.
You'll dig your husband's beets up, too.
All this would have been spared to you
By my true comrade Lämmerslint.

73

Alas, dear sister Gotelint!
1365 The grief must truly pain me deep
If each night through henceforth you sleep,
Against your heart uncouthly pressed
A peasant's coarse, ignoble breast;
His love you'll find a bitter gall!
1370 Weapons! Weapons! This I call
Aloud upon your father's head!
He's not my father, be it said.
And this in very truth I speak;
For when through but the fifteenth week
1375 Within her, mother carried me,
There came to her quite stealthily
A polished, knightly man from court.
So I inherit from such sort,
And from the man who sponsored me[43]
1380 (Blessed may their memories be),
The lofty thoughts and knightly ways
Which I shall show through all my days."

His sister Gotelint then said:
"Neither am I his child! Instead,
1385 There was, I know, another
Who lay once by my mother —
A clever knight, as I've heard say —
While still beneath her heart I lay.
He caught her, on his pleasure bent,
1390 When late at eventide she went
To seek her calves in brush near by.
Thus 'tis, my spirit is so high!

"Dearest brother Schlingdasgeu,
The good Lord fill your heart with joy!"
1395 Thus continued Gotelint,
"Please do your best that Lämmerslint
Be given me as wedded man.
There'll be a crackling in my pan,
My grapes will all be gathered in,
1400 And filled shall be each chest and bin.

The best-brewed beer will then abound,
My meal shall be most finely ground.
If those three sacks my stock increase,
From poverty I'll have release.
1405   With food to eat, good clothes to wear,
No pinch I'll suffer anywhere.
I'll thus have everything in store
That woman wished from man before.
And I can give a husband, too,
1410   All that is a husband's due
From a wife of sturdy kind;
All this he'll in my body find.
For what he wants, I do not lack;
My father merely holds me back.
1415   My body's three times firmer, sure,
Than was my sister's, to endure,
When in marriage she was manned.
And yet, next morning she could stand,
And did not die from overwork!
1420   And so I think I need not shirk;
For death will never lay me low
Unless by some far harder blow.
Brother mine and comrade true,
What I now discuss with you
1425   For love of me to no one say!
I'll go with you the narrow way
That leads through pines up to the hill.
I'll lie by him and do his will.
And know that all of this I'll dare
1430   Spite relatives' and parents' care."

This talk the father did not hear.
Nor was the young girl's mother near.
The brother counseled what to do.
'Twas quickly settled by the two
1435   That she should follow him from thence.
"I'll give you to him, though offense
And pain to father it may bring.

You'll wed my comrade, honoring
Yourself and him by that mere act;
1440 And this will bring the wealth you've lacked.
Now would you see this to the end,
Then back again to you I'll send
A messenger, as guide to you.
You like my friend, he likes you too;
1445 With mutual love, you must succeed
In every undertaken deed.
The wedding plans on me shall rest,
And in your honor every guest
A waist or jacket shall receive.
1450 This shall be done, you may believe.
Do you prepare now, Gotelint!
The same I'll say to Lämmerslint.
God keep you! I must go!" said he,
"I like my host as he does me!
1455 God's blessings, mother, on your head!"

Along his old paths Helmbrecht sped,
And gave at once to Lämmerslint
The pleased consent of Gotelint.
His happiness scarce knew a bound.
1460 He kissed his friend around and round,
Then bowed down low against the wind [44]
That blew to him from Gotelind.

Now hear of violence grim and wild.
Many a widow and her child
1465 In their possessions met with harm,
Were filled with grief and sharp alarm
When the hero, Lämmerslint,
And his betrothed, young Gotelint,
Were both to mount the bridal chair.[45]
1470 What was drunk and eaten there
Was gathered in from all the land;
For as the day drew near to hand
The comrades did not idle stay.
The youths drove in on hoof their prey,

76

1475 And wagons with their stolen freight
They drove in early, drove in late,
To Lämmerslint's parental house.
When famed King Arthur[46] in carouse
Espoused one Guinevere by name,
1480 His celebration was quite tame
Compared with that of Lämmerslind:
These fared on something more than wind!

When everything had been prepared,
Forth Helmbrecht's messenger now fared.
1485 In quickest haste he sped along,
And brought the sister to the throng.

Now when the news reached Lämmerslint
Of the approach of Gotelint,
He went at once to meet her.
1490 Hear how the youth did greet her:
"O, welcome, Lady Gotelint!"
"Reward you God, Sir Lämmerslint!"
Loving glances in exchange
Thick between the two did range.
1495 With each, these glances did occur:
She looked at him, he looked at her.
With well-framed words, and proudly said,
Lämmerslint his bolt now sped
Towards the fair young Gotelint;
1500 And she rewarded Lämmerslint
With words that were as sweet and warm
As her maiden lips could form.

Now we must give young Gotelint
As wife to youthful Lämmerslint,
1505 And we must give young Lämmerslint
As man, in turn, to Gotelint.[47]
A gray-haired man now did arise
Who in the use of words was wise;
Well versed he was in marrying.
1510 He stood both parties in a ring.[48]

Then first he spoke to Lämmerslint:
"And will you take this Gotelint
To be your wife? If so, say 'aye.' "
"Gladly," the young man did reply.
1515 And when he asked the same once more,
He answered "Gladly" as before.
And then he asked a third time still:
"And do you this of your free will?"
He answered: "By my soul and life,
1520 I gladly take her as my wife."
The man then spoke to Gotelint:
"And do you, too, take Lämmerslint
Willingly, your man to be?"
"I do, sir, if God grants him me."
1525 Again he asked the same of her,
Again she said: "I'm willing, sir!"
And then upon his third demand:
"I'm willing, sir, here is my hand!"
They gave away thus Gotelint
1530 To be the wife of Lämmerslint,
And thus they gave young Lämmerslint
To be the man of Gotelint.
And now they sang, the questions put,
And Lämmerslint trod on her foot.[49]
1535 Now for the banquet all is set,
And this much we must not forget:
We must determine and decide
Who serves the bridgroom and the bride.
Schlingdasgeu was marshal gay;[50]
1540 He bulged the horses' hides with hay.
Schluckdenwidder poured the wine.
Höllensack, the next in line,
Seated the guests, both strange and known;
As steward, bright his talent shone.
1545 And he, unsteady, fickle swain,
Rüttelschrein, was chamberlain.
Kuhfrass, kitchener, served the meat;
He gave them all that they could eat,

78

And whether roast, or boiled instead.
1550 Mausdenkelch passed round the bread.
The banquet passed without alarm.
Wolfesgaum and Wolfesdarm
And Wolfesrüssel, at their wish,
Emptied many a well-filled dish,
1555 Drained many a brimming goblet, too,
Ere the wedding feast was through.
Before the lads, food disappeared
With a rapidity quite weird,
As though there'd come a sudden gust
1560 That carried it away like dust.
Each banqueter consumed in haste
All of the foods the stewart placed
Before him — everything he saw.
And did the dogs thereafter gnaw
1565 Meat from the bones when they were through?
No, this a dog could hardly do.
For, as the wise have often said,
A man gulps down his meat and bread
More greedily than e'er before
1570 When death is standing at his door.[51]
And so they now ate greedily —
It was their last festivity —
Last time they sat in merriment
And ate their food to their content.

1575 Then spoke the young bride Gotelint:
"O, woe, belovèd Lämmerslint!
My skin begins to creep with fear!
I feel that strangers must be near
Who on our punishment are bent.
1580 O, father, mother, I repent
I left my home where you two are,
And went away from you so far!
I fear that there will come to me
From Lämmerslinde's gift-sacks three
1585 Dishonor and the greatest harm.

79

I cannot quiet my alarm!
How happy I at home would be!
My spirits weigh so heavily!
My father's poverty I'd bear
1590 Far liefer than the load of care
Which weighs upon my heart today.
How often I have heard them say
That those but little will obtain
Who think of nothing but quick gain
1595 And would too much at once acquire —
That greediness to hell's hot fire
Will hurl one, with its deadly sin,
The yawning pit down deep within.
Too late my penitence may be.
1600 Alas, that I so hastily
Have followed brother Helmbrecht here!
In rue I'll pay for it, I fear!"

The bride thus quickly reasoned out
That she had rather eaten kraut
1605 At home, and as the only dish,
Than Lämmerslint's ill-gotten fish.
Now after they had dined so well
And lingered sitting for a spell,
And when the minstrels' song and play
1610 Had received its meed of pay
From the bridegroom and the bride,
Suddenly they all descried
The justice coming with four men.
How speedily the valiant ten
1615 Quailed at the officers of right!
Into the stove one dived in flight,
While others 'neath the benches crept,
And each one jostled, sprang, and leapt.
Lads who from four had never flown,
1620 By the sheriff's man alone
Were now dragged out by head of hair.
This is the truth that I declare:

A thief, however bold he be,
And though he's slain in one day three,
1625 A man of law he cannot face,
A sheriff brings him to disgrace.
And thus all ten were quickly bound
The selfsame hour that they were found,
With the very strongest bands,
1630 By the sheriff's sturdy hands.
Gotlint, who lost her bridal gown,
Later by a hedge thrown down
Was found, half conscious, half undressed.
She tried to cover each bare breast
1635 With her hands from strangers' sight.
Half dead she was from shock and fright.
Had she had worse to undergo?
Let others tell of that who know!
God is a wonder-worker, true!
1640 The tale reveals that fact to you;
For though a thief may slay a band,
An officer he can't withstand.
When far away one comes in sight
There is a fading of his light,
1645 His ruddy color turns to yellow;
However bold and quick a fellow,
A sheriff, lame, could catch him now.
His bravery and his cunning, how
Upon the instant these are past
1650 When God will have revenge at last!

Now hear the ending of the song.
Hear how the thieves now crept along
With their burdens, to the court,
And there were promptly strung up short.
1655 It brought small joy to Gotelint
When she saw her Lämmerslint,
Two cow-hides bound upon his neck,[52]
Tied to him at the sheriff's beck.
His burden was the least of all;

81

1660 The reason it was made thus small
Was honor to a bridegroom shown;
The others under more did groan.
The brother of the youthful bride
Was made to bear a third rough hide
1665 Before the beadle, luckless boy!
'Twas Helmbrecht, alias Schlingdasgeu!
Each with his load was forced to trudge.
These goods were given to the judge.[53]

They had no advocate at court.
1670 And may God cut his life-span short
Who would extend the span of theirs —
These are my sentiments and prayers!
I know a judge, of such a mind
That if a wolf of wildest kind,
1675 That tore men's cattle for its prey,
If it but gave him ample pay,
For such a bribe he'd set it free,
However venal this might be.

Nine men were strung up in the air.
1680 The sheriff only one did spare.
(It was his tenth — he had that right.)[54]
Schlingdasgeu-Helmbrecht was this wight!

What fate decrees is bound to be!
God seldom spares a man, when he
1685 Does evil deeds he should not do.
In Helmbrecht this we see come true.
To avenge the father, I surmise,
The sheriff pierced out Helmbrecht's eyes.
Nor was the punishment yet through;
1690 For they avenged the mother, too,
By lopping off a hand and foot.[55]
Because he once rude greetings put
To both his parents, now must he
Endure such dire contumely.
1695 To his father thus had spoke Helmbrecht:

82

*"Was hewwt ihr dummer Bur mi seggt?"*
And he called his mother "slut," you know.
These sins now make him undergo
Such torment with his every breath
1700 That he had rather far met death
Than linger on, thus basely maimed,
And drag a life forever shamed.

Now Helmbrecht, blind and crippled thief,
From Gotelint must take his leave
1705 At a forking of the way
With deeper rue than I can say.
To lead him home, the blind thief had,
As guide, a staff and little lad.
With those at home he hoped to stay;
1710 The father drove his son away.
He did not help him in his plight.
Hear what he told the wretched wight!
" *'Dieu vous salue,'* blind sir." Thus short
He spoke. "When once I served at court
1715 I learned exactly what to say
To greet a guest in proper way.
*Min leiwe Blindling,* run along!
For now you have, unless I'm wrong,
What blind youths need, is that not true?
1720 Besides, at court they prize you, too!
This greeting's what you get from me,
For thus I greet blind beggars, see?
What boots this wagging of the tongue?
God knows, sir stranger, blind and young,
1725 My house you must at once vacate.
And if perchance you hesitate,
I'll have my servant give you blows
The like of which, as heaven knows,
Were never rained on blind man's head!
1730 It would be naught but wasted bread
That I should lose on you tonight,
So get you quickly from my sight!"

83

"Oh no, sir, do but let me stay
Beneath your roof till break of day!
1735 Wait! I will tell my name to you;
For God's sake, recognize me, do!"
He answered: "Speak! It's very late!
No time for you to vacillate!
Seek other hosts, and understand,
1740 You'll get no bounty from my hand!"

With deepest pain as well as shame
He told his father then his name:
"Sir, it is I — I am your child!"
"And did they blind the youth so wild
1745 Who bore the name of Schlingdasgeu?
Whom sheriff's threat did not annoy,
Nor judge, nor executioner,
No matter what their numbers were?
Heigh! How much iron you did eat
1750 When seated on your stallion fleet,
Which cost me more than one good cow!
If you go blindly creeping now,
This causes me no wrath or pain.
I grieve for my lost cloth and grain,
1755 So dear has grown for me my bread.
And though you lay from hunger dead
I would not with a crumb give aid!
Let not your going be delayed!
Come this direction never more,
1760 Nor cast your shadow on my door."

Again the blind youth spoke, and said:
"Since your paternal love is dead
And you no further interest take,
You ought still for the dear Lord's sake
1765 To strive the devil to repress.
Then let me, in my great distress,
Within your house's shelter creep.
What from the sick you would not keep,
But give for sake of charity,

84

1770   For love of God, give that to me!
     The country people are my foe.
     Alas, you're hostile, too, I know.
     I cannot any further live
     If you no bit of mercy give!"
1775   Derisively the father spake,
     Although his heart was like to break.
     (The lad was, after all, his own —
     Was of his flesh, and blood, and bone.)
     "Crisscross throughout the world you'd race;
1780   Your horse ne'er went at ambling pace;
     It trotted round and galloped by,
     And many a heart was forced to sigh.
     Such frightfulness was shown by you
     That many peasants, women, too,
1785   Were stripped of everything they had.
     How now with those three dreams, my lad?
     Have they by any chance come true?
     And more still lies in store for you,
     To make you suffer worse than woe!
1790   Before the fourth dream that we know
     Comes true, move on, as bade before!
     Servant, close and bolt the door!
     Tonight I wish my peace and sleep.
     A total stranger I would keep
1795   More willingly, until I'm dead,
     Than give you half a loaf of bread."

     With all the youth had ever done
     He now reproached his eyeless son.
     Repulsed by loathing, he must scoff:
1800   "You, blind man's servant, take him off,
     Despised and hated of the sun!"
     He struck the guide: "And take that one!
     Your master I would give the same
     But for the fact that I'd feel shame
1805   To strike a man of sight bereft.
     I've decency sufficient left

85

That I can still hold back the blow.
But I might change my mind, you know!
Betake yourself, you faithless boor,
1810 In greatest haste forth from my door.
Your suffering is naught to me!"
The mother, not so hard as he,
Passed out, as to a child, a crust.

Off went the blind lad through the dust.
1815 Where'er he went, o'er field or grass,
Each peasant who observed him pass
Cried out to him and to his boy:
"Ha, Helmbrecht, thief, I wish you joy!
Had you, like me, kept to your plow,
1820 You'd not be led round blinded now!"
And thus he suffered, one year through,
Until he died from hanging, too.

I'll tell you how that came, at last.
A peasant saw him going past
1825 As he was seeking out a nest
Within the woods where he could rest.
The man was cutting wood that day
For fire, as is a peasant's way.
'Twas of a morning. Helmbrecht, now,
1830 Had taken his best calving cow —
As fine a beast as one could find;
And now the peasant saw him blind!
He called his neighbors round about
And asked if they would help him out.
1835 "In truth I will," said one with lust,
"I'll shred him into bits of dust
Like those one sees in sunlight fly,
If I'm not stopped by passers-by.
Me and my wife he once roped in
1840 And stripped us to the very skin —
Took every garment we had on;
So now he is my proper pawn."
The third one then spoke up with vim:

"And were there even three of him,
1845 With my sole hand I'd kill all three!
That unclean, thieving devil, he
Once split apart my cellar door
And pillaged all I had in store."
A fourth, who'd been splitting wood for fire,
1850 Shook like a leaf with his desire.
"I'll wring his chicken's neck for spite!
None can deny I have the right!
He stuck my child into a sack
While it lay sleeping on its back;
1855 Wrapped a bed round the little one —
'Twas night when this foul deed was done.
When it awoke and wailed in woe,
He shook it out upon the snow.
Ere morn it surely would have died
1860 Had I not heard it as it cried."
"In faith," a fifth one said in wrath,
"I'm glad he's fallen in our path!
My heart will find a great delight
Today in feasting on his sight.
1865 The villain outraged my poor girl!
And were he thrice as blind, the churl,
I'd hang him to the nearest limb!
And I myself escaped from him
But barely, naked forced to flee.
1870 Though bigger than a house were he,
I'd have revenge on him this day,
Since he has come to creep away
Within this wood so deep and wide."

"Let's after him!" they all then cried,
1875 And turned at twinkling of an eye
Toward Helmbrecht, who had passed on by.
As now they took revenge, they said,
While raining blows upon his head:
"Now save your hood, as best you can!"
1880 And what before the sheriff's man

87

Had left untouched, was this time stripped
And to a hundred tatters ripped.
It was a gruesome thing. They rained
Such hail of blows that there remained
1885 No penny-wide strip of all the hood:
Ring-larks, the gay poll-parrots' brood,
And hawks and doves — the birds had flown
That on the handsome hood were sewn;
They now lay scattered on the ground.
1890 Here a lock of hair was found,
And there a bit of hood: forsooth,
If I have ne'er yet told the truth,
It must by all be understood
I tell it now about the hood,
1895 In what fine bits the thing was torn.
You never saw scalp so forlorn
Upon a head, so bald and bare.
His handsome, flaxen, curly hair,
Of all its dignity bereft,
1900 Bestrewed the earth, and there was left.
But all this punishment was light,
For next they bade the luckless wight
To quickly make his peace with God.
And one of them a little clod
1905 Of earth made haste to break and fetch.[56]
This to the most unworthy wretch
They gave, with charge to use it well
Against the burning fires of hell.
They hanged him to a near-by tree.
1910 And thus the father's dream, you see,
Found fulfillment without fail.
And here must end our little tale.

Let headstrong children everywhere
Who still are in their parents' care
1915 Take a warning from my story.
If théy covet Helmbrecht's glory,
I tell them truly, ere too late,

That they will suffer Helmbrecht's fate.
Upon the streets and on the roads
1920   Men could not safely drive their loads;
Their wagons now in peace may fare,
Since Helmbrecht dangles in the air.

And now look up and round you, too,
And let the simple counsel you.
1925   Take counsel also from the wise.
Does Helmbrecht have, as I surmise,
Young followers who live as he?
If so, they'll little Helmbrechts be.
Never in peace they'll let you fare
1930   Till they, too, dangle in the air.

For him who reads to you this tale
Pray that God's mercy may not fail;
And for the poet pray the same,
Wernher the Gardener is his name.

# DER ARME HEINRICH

Wie Feuer Silber, wie die Flamme Gold,
so prüft der Herr das Herz der Menschenkinder.
*— Sprüche Salomonis*

# DER ARME HEINRICH

A knight there was — so learned [1] he,
That he could read quite easily
In manuscripts and books; the same
Hartmann von Ouwe was by name;
5   He served at Ouwe in vassalage.
His eye ran over many a page
In this and that odd, foreign book;
For thus the knight was wont to look
To see if he could not find aught
10   Wherewith his bad hours might be brought
To pass more lightly, or to find
Other things of such a kind
As to God's honor might redound;
Or whether, with the things he found,
15   He might regale his fellow man.
He now will tell, as best he can,
A tale that in such books he met. [2]
The author's name do not forget,
So that, for all the work applied
20   Hereon, he may not be denied
Reward, however small the meed.
When he has died, whoe'er may read
Or hear some minstrel tell this tale,
Let him beseech God, without fail,
25   For the welfare of the poet's soul.
Who takes forgiveness as his goal
In prayer, for another's sin,
Will best himself forgiveness win.

The story that he now will write,
30   He read once of a certain knight

In Swabia begotten.
In him there was forgotten,
Of manly virtues, none, in truth,
That any noble in his youth,
35  To win full praise, must have.  And he
Was given praise more generously
Than any other in the land.
This Swabian noble had at hand
Great wealth, and was of noble birth.
40  His virtue was of sterling worth.
His wordly goods, howe'er complete,
Could not in any way compete
With the perfection of his birth,
Which measured with the best on earth;
45  And like to birth and worldly good
Were honor, and his knightly mood.

His name was known extensively;
Herr Heinrich he was called; and he
As lord of Ouwe had been born.
50  Within his heart he had forsworn
Falsehood and vulgarity.
He kept his oath most faithfully,
And to his death was steadfast quite.
No deviation from the right
55  His honor soiled, his life defamed.
With fair ambition, too, he aimed
Worldly honors to acquire.
To win these, he could well aspire
With purest virtue, upright truth.
60  He was a flower of manly youth,
Of earthly joys a mirror he,
A diamond of fidelity.
Of breeding, too, a crown indeed;
A refuge for all those in need;
65  For kith and kin a shield was he;
True scales of generosity;
Of this he showed enough, not more.

Upon his back he lightly bore
His load of honors; and, 'tis true,
70   He was a bridge of counsel, too.
He sang of love quite charmingly.[3]
Thus he could win successfully
Men's praise, and gain the highest prize.
He was a courtly knight, and wise.

75   While he of whom this praise is voiced,
The noble Heinrich, thus rejoiced
In honors and in worldly good,
As likewise, too, in happy mood,
And worldly pleasure reveled in
80   (For he above all kith and kin
Was praised, and greater honor earned),
Quite suddenly his bliss was turned,
Cast down he was, and sore distressed.
In him the truth was manifest,
85   Just as in Absalom 'twas shown,
That, namely, the voluptuous crown
Of all things worldly that are sweet
Will often fall beneath one's feet,
Its splendor trodden on and dead,
90   As the Holy Script has said.[4]
Somewhere in the book divine[5]
*Media vita*, runs a line,
*In morte sumus* — words of truth
Which mean that at the height of youth,
95   And while we draw life's sweetest breath,
We're hovering at the brink of death.

This old earth's durability,
Its lasting and its constancy,
Its splendor, pomp and glittering show
100   Have short duration here below.
Of this a candle or a brand
Affords a symbol close at hand;
To ashes, lo, the candle turns,
For while it sheds its light — it burns!

105    We mortals are of fragile stuff!
        We see our laughter oft enough
        Drowned out in tears! This life is fixed
        So that the sweetest sweet is mixed
        With bitterest gall.
110    Our flower must fall[6]
        Just when it seems in finest green.
        In poor Herr Heinrich this was seen:
        Who highest stands in worth and show
        And station on this earth below
115    Oft bears God's scorn, and feels his hand.
        Herr Heinrich fell at his command —
        Fell from his high, illustrious place
        Into a state of dire disgrace:
        He fell a prey to leprosy.[7]
120    Now when it easy grew to see
        The heavy scourge that God had sent
        Upon him as a punishment,
        That marred his limbs and body, then
        He grew repugnant to all men.
125    However pleasing he had been
        Before, and everyone could win,
        He now repulsed all those who might
        Chance to find him in their sight.
        Once long ago this happened, too,
130    To Job, the noble wealthy Jew;
        Him also leprosy once flung,
        As outcast, on a heap of dung.

        Now when poor Heinrich, thus accursed,
        Came to realize for the first
135    That he offended people's sight
        As all do with the leper's blight,
        His bitter grief prohibited
        The patience Job exhibited;
        For Job endured with fortitude
140    And in a most long-suffering mood
        The sickness and the deep disgrace

That he was called upon to face
When forced foul leprosy to bear;
He did it for his soul's welfare.

145 He sang to God, whose praise he voiced;
His soul, though troubled, still rejoiced.
Poor Heinrich this by no means did.
Downcast he was, his face he hid,
His leaping heart now ceased to bound;

150 His buoyant joy was quickly drowned.
His pride was brought now to a fall,
His honey turned to bitter gall.
A peal of thunder, dark as night,
Broke in upon his noonday's height.

155 His heaven with clouds was covered o'er
Till he could see the sun no more.
He could do naught but fret and grieve
That he was now compelled to leave
So many honors far behind.

160 He cursed with all his heart and mind
The hour, now loathed in every way,
When first he saw the light of day.

And yet, one thing there was that brought
Him consolation. 'Twas the thought

165 Which he had heard expressed before:
That this affliction which he bore,
In varying degree endured,
Might, under circumstance, be cured.
With thoughts of this his mind was filled.

170 The voice of hope would not be stilled:
He felt it very possible
His sickness might be curable.
And so he hastened now straightway
To hear what doctors sage might say,

175 At the school of Montpellier.[8]
There he found the poorest cheer;
For the word the doctors gave him
Was: no medicine could save him.

This word his spirit sorely vexed.
180 He hastened to Salerno next,[9]
Where through some doctor's science, he
Hoped soon to make recovery.
He had the best men there behold him.
Of these a leading master told him
185 A most remarkable, strange tale:
He could be cured, made sound and hale,
And yet, his cure he'd never see.
Then Heinrich asked: "How can that be?
Impossible seems what you tell!
190 If in your power, I shall grow well!
No price that you might lay before me
In goods, or work, that might restore me,
But I assure you I would pay."
"Now let your fond hopes fade away,"
195 Thus the master spoke his mind,
"Your illness is of such a kind —
What good that I reveal it? —
That it requires to heal it
A remedy the like of which
200 No mortal man, however rich
Or clever, could obtain,
Or ever hope to gain.
You'll always stay in your condition,
Unless the Lord be your physician.

205 Poor Heinrich answered then. Said he:
"Why do you thus dishearten me?
I have of goods sufficient strength:
Unless you go to such a length
And shirk your art, your duty too,
210 And in addition, unless you
Refuse the gold that I would spend,
I'll make of you so good a friend
That you will cure me willingly."
"You need not doubt I'd willing be,"
215 The master thereupon insisted,

"If such a medicine existed,
That one could find the like for sale,
If one could possibly avail
Himself of it, through riches gain —
220    You would not ask my help in vain.
Unhappily, this cannot be.
In consequence, all help by me
Must unconditionally be denied.
To cure you, there must be supplied
225    A maid, untouched, in honor pure,
And who is willing to endure
A voluntary death for you.
Now people are not wont to do
The like of that, and willingly!
230    You need but this," [10] continued he,
"A maid's heart-blood, to bring you ease;
That would be cure for your disease." [11]

At this strange news poor Heinrich grieved.
For very clearly he perceived
235    How hard 'twould be, a maid to gain
Who would be willing to be slain.
And thus the comfort he had sought
In going there, had come to naught.
From this time on, 'twas plain to see,
240    All thought of his recovery
Was gone. With hope he now must part.
The grief and anguish of his heart
Were so intense, so very great,
He felt but loathing at his fate,
245    That he should any longer live.
He now went home, began to give
Away his goods of every kind,
Quite as the impulse of his mind
And as wise counsel taught him,
250    And as it pleasure brought him.
He wisely carried out his ends;
Endowed the poor among his friends,

99

And strangers, whom he did not know,
He also helped, that God might show
255 Mercy in his soul's salvation.
The monks, too, got a good donation.
Thus Heinrich disengaged himself
With wisdom from all worldly wealth
Save for a clearing in the wood,
260 To which he fled in solitude.
The sad affair, though all his own,
Did not cause grief to him alone.
All lands that knew him mourned him dead,
And strange lands, too, it must be said,
265 Mourned him as well — lands far away,
That knew him only by hearsay.

This forest clearing isolated
Was at the time still cultivated
By a peasant, freeborn[12] and content,
270 Who very seldom underwent
Any great discomfort, such
As other peasants suffered much,
Who had worse overlords to bear,
Since these latter did not spare
275 Them hard exactions or commands.[13]
Whate'er was done by this man's hands
For Heinrich, that appealed to him
As quite enough. He shielded him
So that he suffered, and his farm,
280 From no one, violence or harm.
Hence it was, that far around
No man so prosperous could be found.

Away from home, then, Heinrich fared,
And to his peasant he repaired.
285 His kindness, ere he thus was blighted,
How splendidly 'twas now requited,
How amply did he benefit!
What came on him through Heinrich, it
Now seemed by no means imposition.

290 It was the peasant's disposition
    For Heinrich willingly to bear
    All the work and all the care
    That fell on him.  For him he tried
    Abundant comfort to provide.

295 The peasant, with God's aid, had spent
    A life both cleanly and content.
    He had muscles steeled by industry,
    And a wife of great activity.
    Pretty children were his, beside,
300 The like of which are a father's pride.
    And the peasant also had, they say,[14]
    A daughter 'mong his children gay,
    A child about the age of eight,[15]
    But in her bearing full sedate;
305 In impulse so mature and kind
    That it was never in her mind
    To leave her master.  For his favor
    And the words of thanks he gave her,
    She waited on him everywhere
310 With the most devoted care.
    So charming, too, she is reputed
    To have been, that she was suited
    To be the daughter of a king.

315 The others of the household ring,[16]
    As far as proper was, and right,
    May have inclined to shun his sight.
    But she ran to him constantly,
    And wanted nowhere else to be.
320 She was his pastime solely.
    She had turned her young heart wholly
    To him in childish purity,
    In goodness and in loyalty;
    And at all times she chose her seat
325 Down at her lord and master's feet.
    With sweet attentions she supplied
    His needs, and stayed close to his side.

And he in turn gave her much joy
With every kind of gift and toy;
330 All that seemed suited to her — nay,
And more, he gave her for her play.
That children are so quickly made
To feel accustomed, was an aid.
335 Whatever was for sale, he bought;
Mirrors, ribbons; and he sought
What pleases children's hearts — such things
As pretty girdles, finger rings.
With gifts like these it came to pass,
340 So intimate became the lass,
He often called her "little spouse,"
And very seldom in the house
She let him solitude endure.
He knew that she was very pure.
345 Much as the childish gifts he gave
Induced the maid thus to behave,
Her gift from God, a spirit sweet,
Did most to make her charm complete.

So thus she served, thus errands ran.
350 When Heinrich now, unhappy man,
Had dwelt there some three years or so,
And God had racked with torture slow
His limbs, and filled with pain his life,
One day, the peasant and his wife
355 And their young child, the little maid
Of whom above so much is said,
With busied hands that idled not,
Sat by their lord, and mourned his lot.
His sorrow needs must give them pain.
360 They bore the fear, by no means vain,
That once their master's death arrived
They would be harmed, and e'en deprived
Of honors, forced with goods to part,
365 By some new lord of harder heart.
Thus far their conversation ran,

And at this point the farming man
Addressed his lord inquiringly:

"Dear lord and master mine," said he,
370 "I would not your kind patience task,
Still there is something I would ask.
Though to Salerno you went round,
Where master-doctors so abound,
How does it happen, tell us, please,
375 That in the cure of your disease
No doctor any aid has lent?
This rouses my astonishment!"
At that poor Heinrich's lips let part
A sigh that came from out his heart
380 In bitter grief. His words were spoken
As if by pain his heart were broken,
As were the sighs that heaved his breast.

"Some way, perhaps, this bitter jest
At heaven's hand I have deserved;
385 For, as you doubtless have observed,
Wide open stood my gate, my door,
To worldly pleasures heretofore,
And none of all my kind, I'd say,
Loved more to have his will and way.
390 And yet, this was not so to be,
For naught I had belonged to me.
I gave to him but little heed
Whose grace permitted me to lead
A life of so much ease and good.
395 And thus it was that my heart stood
As all men's hearts do, fooled by earth,
Whose intellects believe that worth,
And goods, and honor, we possess
Aside from God's great kindliness.
400 This vain belief deceived me, too.
I looked but little on him, who
Bestowed upon me by his grace
My worldly goods and honored place.

Now when my thoughtlessness of late
405   Vexed the Keeper of the Gate,[17]
He closed against me Fortune's door,
And I shall enter it no more.
For this I blame my own dull mind.
God sent me sickness of a kind
410   That no one can effect a cure.
This punishment I must endure.
By evil men I am abhorred,
And by the good I am ignored.
If worthless men look down on me,
415   I must, alas, more worthless be.
Their littleness is clear as day,
Because they turn their eyes away.
In you, good friend, and you alone,
Has faithful loyalty been shown:
420   You keep me in my leprosy,
And do not turn away to flee.
But now, although you shun me not,
Though you're the only friend I've got,
And though your weal is based on me,
425   You well could bear my end to see!
Whose worthlessness, whose bitter need
Was ever quite so great indeed?
I was your master heretofore —
I'm now a beggar at your door.
430   You're buying, friend, eternal life —
You, my "spouse," [18] and your good wife.
Salvation you will surely win
Because you take me, sick one, in.
What you have asked so sadly
435   I'll answer now right gladly.
I could not at Salerno find
A single man who was inclined
To take my case into his care;
He would not, neither did he dare.
440   For, in order that I might
Be restored to health aright,

Such a thing must needs be done,
No mortal person could be won
To do it. Do not feel surprise,
445 But I was told not otherwise
Than that I'd have to find, unspoiled,
A maid, whose honor was unsoiled,
And also one who'd willing be
To undergo her death for me,
450 Deep to her heart to let them cut;
For naught, said they, would cure me but
The blood from out the maiden's heart.
That any living maid would part
With life — that she would willingly
455 Endure her death to succor me,
That is impossible indeed;
Hence I must bear my shameful need
Without a hope until my end.
May God the same now quickly send!"

Now what between the men occurred,
460 The maiden pure had also heard.
For the little girl so sweet
Was holding her loved master's feet
In her lap with gentle care.
One might well indeed compare
465 The childlike goodness on her part
With the goodness of an angel's heart.
What her lord had had to tell
She listened to, and marked it well.
She cherished every word he said
470 Until that night they went to bed.
When at her parents' feet she lay
(For they were wont to sleep that way),
And the two had gone to sleep,
The little maiden could not keep
475 Choked back the sighs that sought relief.
The knowledge of her master's grief
Aroused her pity, caused her pain,

Until her tears, which fell like rain,
Made wet her sleeping parents feet.
480 Thus they were roused by the maiden sweet.

The parents, thus awaked from sleep
Because they felt their daughter weep,
Asked what was wrong, what grieved her so,
If any care suppressed, or woe,
485 Made her lament in such a way.
The little daughter would not say,
Until her father urged her, and
With both entreaty and command
Asked her to tell what it might be.
490 She said: "You well may grieve with me.
What should more sorrow for us make
Than worry for our master's sake?
That we shall lose him now, we know,
And with him, must we not forego
495 Our standing and material gain?
Oh, nevermore shall we obtain
So good a master! None e'er was,
Who'd treat us as Herr Heinrich does!"

They answered: "Daughter, though you're right,
500 Not all your weeping through the night,
Nor all our grief, will help a hair!
So, dearest child, give o'er your care!
We're both as grieved as you can be.
Alas, unfortunately, we
505 Can in no fashion help him out.
The hand of God one cannot flout.
Had another put this on him,
We'd cry our curse upon him."

They silenced thus their daughter, who
510 Remained quite sad the whole night through,
As well, too, all the following day.
Whatever they could do or say,
Her mind and heart remained quite bent

On this, till they next evening went
515  To seek as usual their bed.
When she had laid her little head
In its wonted resting-place,
Again she bathed her little face
In a flood of tears; for she
520  Bore within her secretly,
Close hidden in her heart, much more
Of goodness than I've seen before.
I've seen her equal never.
What child could match her ever?
525  For she resolved within the night
That if she lived to see the light
Of morning, she would surely give
Her life, to let her master live.

This thought now made her very
530  Light-hearted, almost merry.
She had no care of any kind,
Save for a fear that plagued her mind:
That when to Heinrich she imparted
Her plan, he would be too faint-hearted;
535  And that, when she had told all three,
She would not very easily
Receive from them permission
To fulfill the strange condition.

Her agitation once more high,
540  Again her parents were thereby
Awakened from their sleep outright,
As had occurred the previous night.
They sat bolt-upright in their bed.
"What troubles you, dear child?" they said.
545  "You're very foolish, thus in vain
To weigh your spirits down with pain
Borrowed from your master's grief,
To which no soul can bring relief.
Let us sleep!" the parents told her,
550  And the two began to scold her.

They asked her what her mourning would
Avail her, in that no one could
The sickness cure, or make more mild.
Thus they thought the sweet young child
555 To silence, and her grief to still.
They little knew her firm-set will!

The maiden then made answer thus:
"As our master said to us,
To make him well there is a way;
560 And even though you say me nay,
I'll be his cure.  I am a maid,
And I am ready, unafraid,
Before I see our master dead,
To die myself, and in his stead."

565 With grief and consternation
The girl's strange conversation
Filled the parents of the child.
That she should drop such notions wild
The father thereupon besought
570 His girl, and told her that she ought
Not promise such a thing to do,
Because she'd not be able to.

"You're but a little child," said he,
"And have too great a loyalty
575 In these things you talk about.
You could never carry out
What you've asserted to us here!
Death you've never yet been near.
If the time once came at last
580 When all saving you was past,
And you surely had to die,
Then how hard you'd long, and try
To stay still in your living state.
You'd then be in an evil strait!
585 Hold your little tongue therefore
From this time on, and talk no more!

If again your lips let part
Such talk, your skin shall surely smart!"

Thus he fancied he might yet
590 By entreaty and by threat
Silence her: it was in vain.
Thus she answered him again:

"I am but young; still, I possess
Enough of mind, that ne'ertheless
595 I know, from hearsay, that one's death —
The yielding up of one's last breath —
Is grim, and hard, and bitter, too;
Yet those who live a long life through,
Filled out with toil and labor — such
600 Find their reward by no means much.
One may in struggle here engage,
And foster to a ripe old age
His body, through life's hard travail,
Yet in the end death will prevail.
605 But if his soul is lost in sin,
'Twere better he had never been.
I've reached the point, in early days
(For which I'll ever sing God's praise)
That I, to win eternal life,
610 Will give my body to the knife.
Don't spoil it for me," added she,
"For both of you, as well as me
Myself I'd thereby greatly serve.
For I, alone — I can preserve
615 You both, from damage, grief and pain,
As herewith I shall now explain:
You have both goods and honor[19] too.
To our kind master this is due.
No grievous word has he once spoken,
620 Nor his kindness to you ever broken.
The while he lives, you may be sure
That your good fortune will endure.
But if we let our master die,

Our own destruction stands hard by.
625  Let me preserve for us the man,
In the one sure way I can,
That we may live through him. Now see,
Grant my will, for it must be!"

Abundant tears the mother shed
630  To see her earnestness. She said:
"Daughter, dearest child, recall
How great my labors were, and all
That for your sake I did endure!
Let my reward be not so poor
635  As in these words I hear you say,
Or you will grieve my heart away.
Moderate your speech a bit,
Or you will forfeit soon by it
Your salvation at God's hand.
640  Think you no more of his command?
He has ordered, well you know,
That one should love and honor show
One's mother and one's father toward;
And promised, as return reward,
645  Deliv'rance of the soul from hell,
And here on earth long life as well.
You say, the thing you want to do
Is give your life to help us two.
But what you'd do for us indeed
650  Is, blight our lives by such a deed!
If in our lives we pleasure take,
It's due to you, and for your sake.
652a  What boots us life or goods of earth,[16]
652b  What courage would we have, or mirth,
652c  If we were robbed of you tomorrow?
652d  You should not cause us such great sorrow!
You ought to be, dear daughter mine,
To both of us a joy divine,
654a  Our love, that brings no grief, a sight
654b  That's our supremest eyes' delight,

655 A rapture we may revel in,
A flower to all your kith and kin,
A staff, to steady age's hand.
And if you cause us soon to stand
Where you lie buried neath the sod,
660 Then from the favor of your God
Forevermore you'll be shut out:
*That's* what you'd do for us, no doubt!
662a If you'd be good, then, daughter dear,
662b For love of God don't let us hear
662c Plans like this that we have heard,
662d Or talk, such as has just occurred!"

"Mother, I have confidence,"
She said, "in you and father; hence
665 I know you'll show me all forbearance
And kindness, such as loving parents
Show their child in every way.
Till now, you've shown me every day
Nothing but such kindliness.
670 By your favor I possess
A pretty form and winning ways.
Both men and women sing my praise.
Those who see me all declare
That never maiden quite so fair
675 Have they beheld their whole life through.
To whom but you must thanks fall due,
After God? To no one, nay.
Hence I gladly should obey
Each command that you express;
680 How right this is, I must confess!
Blessed woman, mother, wife,[20]
Since my very soul and life
Is due your kindly disposition,
Oh let it be with your permission
685 That both of these I sever
From the Evil One forever,
And join God, through the doctor's knife!

111

For as you know, this earthly life
Is lived all at the poor soul's cost.
690 But up to now, no worldly lust
Has touched me, as you know quite well,
The like of which leads down to hell.
To God I voice my thanks and praise
That in my young and childish days
695 He has the judgment to me lent,
So that but little heed I've spent
On this frail life which can't endure.
I wish to give myself, thus pure,
To God, to enter in his fold.
700 I fear, if I should e'er grow old,
That I'd be drawn beneath the feet
Of earthly things that taste so sweet,
Just as earth's sweetness has deceived
So many, who in it believed.
705 From God my life might thus be bent.
To God I therefore must lament
That I must live till morning light.
The world affords me small delight.
Its greatest joy proves heavy grief
710 (Life forces one to this belief),
Its sweet reward is bitter need,
Its long life is but death indeed.
And naught is certain that we know,
But joy today, tomorrow woe,
715 With death at last as life's ill gain.
We're granted but a path of pain.
One's wealth cannot protect, nor birth,
Nor beauty, courage, strength, nor worth.
Nor does one's virtue help one, nor
720 One's honor save one, any more
Than lack of virtue or good birth.
Our life and youth upon this earth
Is only mist, of dust a sheaf;
Our firmness trembles like a leaf.
725 He is a fool, a dupe of sin

Who grasps the vaporous mist within
(Whichever gender of our kind),
Who cannot keep this truth in mind,
And has for earth a hankering tongue.
730 For o'er a heap of rotten dung
The carpet here for us is spread.
Whoe'er is by his sight misled
To everlasting hell is lost,
And he must pay no lesser cost
735 Than soul and body — both of these.
Be mindful, blessed woman, please,
Of motherly fidelity,
And moderate the grief for me
That you are feeling for my sake.
740 Let father, too, good counsel take.
Well I know, he never would
Begrudge salvation, he's so good!
He recognizes well and true
That I for no long time to you
745 Would any lasting pleasure give,
Even though I long should live.
If unmarried I should be,
Two years perhaps, perchance for three,
Our master maybe will have died;
750 And such great need may then betide
Us all, you can't allow me
For marriage any dowry
The like which parents always give.
So wretchedly I then should live,
755 That death far rather I would seek!
Of need like this let us not speak;
Assuming, then, that all goes well,
And that for quite a lengthy spell
Our lord continues on to live,
760 Till you my hand in marriage give
To a farmer — one of riches vaunted —
That would be quite what you wanted.
You'd think me lucky, wouldn't you?

My spirits take a different view!
765 If I come to love him, that were need.
To hate him, that were death indeed!
And thus, I'll always have but grief,
And be shut off, without relief,
From any ease or peace of mind,
770 With affairs of every kind
Which confuse a wife
And spoil her joy in life.
Let me enjoy the great supply
Which fails one never, ne'er runs dry.
775 A Farmer[21] seeks me for his wife
To whom I gladly yield my life.
O, give me to him then, betide,
And all my wants will be supplied.
His plow moves steadily indeed,
780 His yard is stored for every need.
His horses, cattle, never die,
With him the children never cry.
It never grows too hot or cold,
And no one ever waxes old.
785 The older ones grow younger.
There is no thirst nor hunger.
There is no grief of any kind,
And joy in work is all you find.
This Farmer will my refuge be.
790 From all the farms I wish to flee,
Where hail and lightning savage
And evil flood-waves ravage;
Where only struggling toil is found;
And when one's worked the whole year round,
795 All that's been accomplished may
Be wiped out in half a day.
I leave such farming for the worse,
And I pronounce on it my curse.
You have a proper love for me.
800 Now I'll be very glad to see
That love for me in love's own guise.

If you will only both be wise,
And know to treat me properly,
And if you will but grant to me
805 Honor, and as well great wealth,
Permit that I devote myself
Now to Jesus Christ our Lord,
Whose grace is always constant toward
Us all, and never perishes.
810 For my poor self he cherishes
A love that measures quite as great
As for a queen of high estate.
Through fault of mine I'll never
Part with your favor, ever —
815 Adding wisely: If God will!
For the Lord commands me still
To give obedience to you two,
Because I have my life from you.
I do this very willingly.
820 But then, again, my loyalty
To my own self I ought not break.
The wise I've heard the statement make:
Who pleases others at such cost
That his own happiness is lost,
825 Who crowns another person's head,
Himself dishonoring instead,
His loyalty is too much quite!
Gladly, in so far as right,
I'll render you my loyalty;
830 But the greatest I must render me!
If from my welfare you would keep
Me, I would rather have you weep
For me, than that I should forego
The duty that to me I owe,
835 To my own self! I wish to fare
To that good land without a care,
Where joys are full and know no pain.
Your other children will remain
To you; let these your comfort be;

840 Console yourselves for loss of me.
    None can cause me now to swerve
    From the course I know will serve
    My lord and master, and me, too.
    Forsooth, dear mother, did not you
845 Lament, and say a while ago
    That it would cause you grief and woe
    If you should stand upon the plot
    Where I lay buried? You will not!
    All this you will be spared; for know,
850 The place where to my death I go
    No one will ever let you see:
    At far Salerno it will be.
852a There, all four of us, indeed,
852b My death will raise above all need.
    My death will heal us all — me too,
    Me better than the rest of you."

855 When they saw the girl so chaste
    To voluntary death thus haste,
    And speak thus wise, above her station,
    Transcending human limitation,
    The parents started to surmise
860 That all this courage, these words wise
    Surely could not have been shown
    By an unguided child alone;
    That the Holy Ghost had lent
    His guidance to her sentiment,
865 Who also for Saint Nicholas cared [22]
    Before he from his cradle fared,
    And to him the wisdom taught
    To turn to God, as mortals ought,
    His desire and childish heart.
870 With all goodness on their part,
    They resolved now that they would not
    Turn their daughter — that they should not —
    From that on which her soul was bent;
    They saw her will from God was sent.

875 Grief benumbed their very life,
As the peasant and his wife
On their bed sat, and forgot,
From love of her they had begot,
How to speak, or think a thought,
880 At the blow the night had brought
So suddenly, within an hour.
It lay no more in either's power
To speak a word or answer back.
Torturing pains began to rack
885 The mother, caused by grief and care;
And thus the two of them sat there,
Saddened and dejected,
Until they recollected
What might be in their grief of use.
890 They did not wish to disabuse
Her of her will, or frustrate it;
So nothing seemed so good and fit
As finally to acquiesce.
They could not, they must needs confess,
895 Lose her in a better way.
Now if they showed displeasure, they
Might likely see the tie destroyed
Which with their master they enjoyed,
Yet profit by it not a whit.
900 And so they made the best of it;
Their willingness at last they voiced,
And said to her that they rejoiced.

At that the pure young maid was gay,
And when the morn had scarce turned gray,
905 Ran to her sleeping master's bed.
His "little spouse" then called, and said
To Heinrich: "Sir, are you awake?"
"Yes, little spouse, but goodness sake,
Why in such early hours astir?"
910 "I've been compelled to do it, sir,
Because your illness grieves me so!"

"Yes, little spouse," he said, "I know.
You show this in your every way,
And God's reward will be your pay.
915 But naught can help me, that is sure!"
"In truth, dear master mine, a cure
With you is possible indeed!
Since things stand thus as to your need,
That for assistance there's a way,
920 I shall not wait a single day.
Master, you yourself have said
That if you could obtain a maid
Who for you would death endure,
Her sacrifice would be your cure.
925 That maiden I myself shall be.
Your life's worth more than mine to me!"

Her master thanked her deeply then
For this kind will she showed him; when
In both his eyes the maid could see
930 The tears that gathered silently.
Said he: "My spouse, dear little thing,
To die is not light suffering,
As you have evidently thought!
To me you have conviction brought
935 That you would help me if you might,
And that must satisfy me quite.
I recognize your spirit sweet;
Your will is purity complete;
I may not covet more from you.
940 And you can never really do
The thing that you have offered me.
For what you've shown of loyalty
May God's reward be of the best.
It would be the people's jest
945 If I should now my recourse make
To remedies that I might take,
And if the sole effect of these
Were but continuance of disease.

You're like all children, spouse, I'd say —
950  They act in an impulsive way.
Every notion they have had,
Whether good, or whether bad,
On doing it they are intent,
But afterward they soon repent.
955  Little partner, this is how
You feel about the matter now.
If one should take you at your word,
Once the first steps had occurred,
You'd rue it, and you'd be afraid."
960  He then requested of the maid
That she should weigh the matter still.
He said: "You know, your parents will
Scarcely wish to let you go,
Nor could I pleasure in their woe
965  Who've been so kind in every wise.
What your parents both advise,
Little wife, that you must do!"
And hereupon he laughed then, too,
For little did he then foresee
970  What, after all, soon came to be.

So they spoke to one another.
The father and the mother
Then said: "Loved lord, our very own,
More love and honor you have shown
975  To us than ever was our due.
Such love were ill bestowed by you
If we did not repay in kind.
Our little girl is of a mind
To die to cure your leprosy,
980  And we accede most willingly.
980a  She merits all our gratitude.
980b  With her 'tis no quick-passing mood;
It's now three days ago today
Our daughter sought in every way
Our permission to acquire.

And now we've granted her desire.
985 God grant to you, through her, your cure!
For you, her loss we shall endure."

When now his little spouse so pure
Strove thus to die to work his cure,
Her serious purpose being plain,
990 There was much distress and pain.
Of grief their bearing made confession;
And now all kinds of dire oppression
Arose to harass and perturb,
And bonds of friendship to disturb.
995 Although they had not made complaint,
Her parents wept without restraint;
And well the two might weep, indeed,
In prospect of their loved child's deed.
The master, too, had now begun
1000 To think, more than he yet had done,
Of the little maiden's loyalty;
And sad he felt to such degree,
He bitterly began to weep.
From gravest doubt he could not keep,
1005 Whether or not the thing were one
He had not better leave undone.
With tears of fear the maid responded,
Because she thought that he desponded.

Thus all were sad, their pleasure dead;
1010 No word of thanks did they wish said.
At last their stricken master kind,
Poor Heinrich, now made up his mind.
And he began most gratefully
To say his thanks to them, all three,
1015 For the devotion they displayed.
Elated was the little maid
That Heinrich yielded thus to her.
At the earliest date it could occur,
For Salerno he prepared with speed
1020 Everything the girl might need.

120

Herr Heinrich speedily now chose
A pretty horse and velvet clothes
The like of which she'd ne'er worn yet;
Ermine he made haste to get,
1025  And a sable — best he could acquire —
Such was the little girl's attire.

Now who in words could half express
The sorrow and the bitterness
The deep, grim grief the mother bore,
1030  The pain the father's spirit wore?
It would have been a sad leave-taking,
It would indeed have been heart-breaking,
As now they sent their child away
To death — so sound in every way —
1035  And ne'er to see the girl again,
Had God not softened them their pain,
Through his goodness pure and mild,
Which had caused the sweet young child
The resolution to embrace,
1040  Thus willingly her death to face.
They had been led to do their part,
And he had taken from their heart
All lament, all weight from her;
For else, a miracle it were
1045  That their hearts withstood the strain.
God transformed to love their pain,
And so they felt no more heart-breaking
At their loved child's undertaking.

Toward Salerno thus she went,
1050  Very joyous and content —
The maiden with her lord. And now
What could trouble her fair brow
Except the distance they confronted,
Which postponed the death she wanted?
1055  Now when he'd brought her overland
And reached his goal as he had planned,
And stood before the doctor's door,

Whom he'd consulted once before,
To him with joy Herr Heinrich said
1060 That he had brought him such a maid
As he had bidden him to win.
With that, he let the maiden in.

The doctor couldn't think it true.
He asked of her: "Dear child, have you
1065 Willed this yourself, as he has said,
Or has your will been somehow led
Or forced, that you should wish to die?"
To this the maiden made reply,
The resolution on her part
1070 Was formed alone, within her heart.

Her words great wonderment supplied.
The doctor led the girl aside,
Where he entreated her to say
If her lord in any way
1075 Had forced her will by word or deed.
"Child," he said, "there's gravest need
That you should reconsider well.
The reason why to you I'll tell.
If you've been influenced, and rue it —
1080 If you do not gladly do it —
Then you will die indeed, but it
Will avail us not a whit!
Hide not your will, whate'er you do.
I'll tell you what will happen you:
1085 I'll strip you to the very skin,
To your shame and your chagrin.
You'll be ashamed quite rightfully,
For to my eyes you'll naked be.
I'll bind your limbs beyond appeal.
1090 If pity for yourself you feel,
Bethink these pains now, at the start!
I'll cut you to the very heart,
And tear it from your breast so fair.
Little lady, now declare

1095 Your full desire, for I must know.
A child has never felt such woe
As I'll inflict on you. You'll rue it!
Myself, I almost fear to do it;
I hate to be the instrument.
1100 Bethink yourself, then, and repent.
If by a hair you rue the pain,
My labor will be spent in vain;
In vain, too, all that you've endured."
Again he solemnly adjured
1105 Her, if not fully confident,
To turn back yet from her strange bent.

The maiden laughingly replied —
Because the hope seemed justified
This very day might see her gain
1110 Complete release from earthly pain —
"God bless you, sir! For kind you are
That you have told to me thus far,
Thus unreserved, the fullest truth.
I *am* discouraged, sir, forsooth!
1115 A doubt assails me suddenly,
And I'll confess quite openly
What sort of doubt your words inspired,
That I have suddenly acquired.
I fear our goal may in a trice,
1120 And through your own great cowardice
Be doomed to stay beyond our reach.
A woman might indulge such speech!
You are a comrade of the hare!
Far too much anxious fear you bear,
1125 Because to die I've shown the will.
However great may be your skill,
You act but ill, I must confess!
A woman I, yet strength possess.
If now you dare to cut, be sure
1130 I dare the cutting to endure.
The talk of fearful deeds to do

Which you've described as waiting you,
I've listened to and felt no fear.
I never would have journeyed here
1135   Had I not known that I am stable
Enough in spirit, that I'm able
To endure each hard condition.
And I may say, with your permission,
Fear's color from my face has fled.
1140   So firm a will has come instead,
That I as eagerly here stand
As though we had a dance at hand.
Pain's not so great that I must face
But 'twill, in one short daytime's space
1145   Upon me soon expended be.
It would by no means seem to me
Too great a price for me to give
That I may everlasting live,
Yea, live a life that never ends.
1150   As far as on my will depends,
No longer can you say me nay,
If you believe that in this way
You can my master's health restore,
And give me life forevermore.
1155   In God's name do it then, this hour!
Display your master's skill and power.
I feel a strong allurement to it.
I know quite well in whom I do it:
In the name of one, whose eyes
1160   Are very quick to recognize
A service, which is e'er repaid.
I know that he himself has said:
Who gives most service to his Lord
Will have from him the most reward.[23]
1165   Hence this bitter death I'll take
As sweetest torture for his sake,
For sure reward. If I forewent
The crown in heaven on which I'm bent,
I'd surely show a foolish mind,

1170     For here, I am of lowly kind."

       Now when he saw the one he'd taken
       For so slight, could not be shaken,
       He led her quickly back again
       To the stricken, leprous man.
1175     To him the doctor then spoke thus:
       "The fear no more need trouble us,
       Your maid might not prove remedy!
       And now, you well may joyous be.
       I'll work your cure without delay!"
1180     At once he led the maid away
       In his chamber, secretly,
       Where her master could not see.
       He closed the door against his face,
       And shoved the door-bolt into place,
1185     That Heinrich might not apprehend
       The horrors of the maiden's end.

       In his workroom, round about
       Elaborately fitted out
       And stocked with medicines, he bade
1190     The expectant little maid
       Immediately to undress.
       At this she felt but joyfulness.
       She stripped off all the clothes she wore,
       And soon no single garment bore.
1195     But she, though stripped for him to see,
       Felt shamed by it in no degree.

       Now when he saw her thus undressed,
       The doctor in his heart confessed
       That maidens on this earth thus fair
1200     And chaste, must truly be most rare.
       She roused his pity very much.
       His sympathy for her was such
       That almost he was quite unnerved.
       The good young maiden now observed
1205     A big, tall table standing by.

On it the master bade her lie.
He bound her fast with many a band.
And now he wielded in his hand
A great sharp knife that lay in place,
1210 Which he employed in such a case.
The knife was long and shining, but
By no means it so keenly cut
As he required of it.  Since she
Was not to make recovery,
1215 He wished to ease her dying breath,
And do her gently to her death.

Within his reach there lay a hone,
The doctor's finest whetting stone.
Now he rubbed the knife blade on it,
1220 Whetting leisurely upon it,
To sharpen it.  When this occurred,
The sound outside poor Heinrich heard
(He who soon her joy disturbed),
While waiting at the door perturbed.
1225 It wakened in him grief and pain
That he should see her ne'er again
Alive, for she was now to die.
He now began to seek and spy
Until, in the partition thin
1230 He found a hole that opened in.
He saw her, looking through the crack,
Naked, tied upon her back.
Her body with rare beauty shone.
He looked at it, then at his own,
1235 Until a change of mind he had;
The cure appeared to him as bad
That he was trying to work out.
Poor Heinrich's will turned quite about.
The old desire that he had nursed
1240 Was to unselfishness reversed.

Her beauty having thus beheld,
These words from Heinrich's lips now welled:

"Stupid thoughts your mind must fill
That you, without the good Lord's will
1245 (Against whom none may have his way),
Should seek to live a single day!
You know not what you are about,
Surely die you must, beyond a doubt,
That now you do not willing live
1250 This shameful life that God doth give,
To test, if you can patience show.
And what is more, you do not know
If this child's death will work a cure.
What God lays on you to endure,
Accept, and bear in loyalty!
This dear child's death I will not see!"

He, hesitating not at all,
Began to knock upon the wall,
Demanding that he be let in.
1260 The master answered with chagrin:
"I'm busy! And I have no leisure
Just now, to listen to your pleasure!"
"But master! Listen! Speak with me!"
"No," he replied, "that cannot be!
1265 Once through, I'll open up the door."
"No, doctor, speak with me before!"
"Speak, if you must, but through the wall."
"It's not what you surmise at all!"

He opened thereupon to him,
1270 And Heinrich entered quickly in.
Standing by the bound girl's head,
To the master he then said:
"This maiden is so charming,
I can't endure her harming.
1275 Her death I cannot, will not see!
God's will must take its course with me.
Please let her up again straightway!
Whatever I agreed to pay,
The silver, I shall gladly give;

127

1280 But you must let the maiden live!"

When the maiden, who had willed
To die, saw she would not be killed,
Her heart was grieved most mightily.
She broke through all propriety.
1285 Quite wrathfully she tore her hair.
Her gestures spoke of such despair
That no one could have seen the sight
But that he would have wept outright.
She cried and called out bitterly:
1290 "Oh, woe, alas! Oh, woe is me!
What loss to me this change will cost;
For have I not in this way lost
The heavenly crown I struggled toward?
It would have been my great reward,
1295 Given for my pain and need.
Alas, now am I dead indeed!
Almighty Christ, how great a cost!
What honors to us both are lost,
Both to my master and to me!
1300 He'll be without, as well as me,
The honors for us each intended.
If this had only but been ended,
His body would then have been cured,
And my eternal life insured!"

1305 Thus for her death she interceded,
But feared, however much she pleaded,
Her prayer would be no longer heard.
Since neither of the two men stirred,
A stern upbraiding she began:
1310 "I must atone, as best I can,
My master's weak despondency.
They have not told the truth to me,
This much I now perceive full well!
I've always heard the people tell
1315 How you were upright, good, and kind,
With a man's firm will and mind.

128

So help me God, the people lied!
The world's deceived in you!" she cried.
"You always were, beyond a doubt,
1320 An arrant coward, out and out!
It's proven by this very thing.
Although I dare the suffering,
You do not dare to let me try!
For what good reason, master — why
1325 Did you take fright when I was bound?
An ample wall enclosed me round,
It shut you out and shut me in.
Is then your courage made so thin
You can't endure another's end?
1330 I promise and assure you, friend,
None else you'll ever find who would
Provide for you the cure that's good."

Howevermuch she stormed at last,
Entreated, and reproaches cast,
1335 It helped her not; her high aims fell,
She had to stay alive and well.
Whate'er reproach her lips let fall,
Poor Heinrich simply took it all
Like a knight of piety,
1340 With a flawless courtesy,
Whose breeding never failed. The guest,
Poor Heinrich, doomed to stay unblessed,
Now reclothed his little maid,
And when the doctor had been paid,
1345 As at the start he had agreed,
He departed then with speed
For his homeland; well he knew
What he, arrived there, must live through:
That once at home, he'd surely find
1350 From common mouth and common mind
Invective — mockery everywhere.
Before God's throne he laid the care.
By now the little maid forlorn

From grief and weeping was so worn,
1355   That she near died. Her steadfastness
Was recognized, and her distress,
By *Cordis Scrutator*,[24]
Before whose eyes the secret door
Of no one's heart is closed complete.
1360   Since God now, in his wisdom sweet,
Heeding what he deemed their best,
Had put the two to this great test,
As thorough and as searching quite
As once tried Job in all his might,
1365   Now holy Jesus Christ above
Showed how he cherishes in love
Compassion and fidelity:
From all their grief he set them free;
Before a single day went round,
1370   He made poor Heinrich clean and sound.

Thus, journeying his homeland toward,
Nursed by Jesus Christ the Lord,
Our good Herr Heinrich steadily
Began to cast his leprosy;
1375   His handsomeness returned to him,
And he grew sound in every limb.
It seemed by years he younger grew.
The greatest joy their spirits knew.
By messenger, sent on ahead,
1380   To those at home the news he sped
Of this good fortune on his part,
So that each friend within his heart
Might at this turn of things delight.
All those who knew him must with right
1385   Take pleasure in this mercy, shown
By God, to one who was their own.

The best among his friends — the few
Who knew when Heinrich would be due,
Went three days toward him on his course,[25]
1390   Some on foot and some on horse,

*From "Album du Musée de sculpture comparée," by P. Frantz Marcou, by permission of Ch. Massin & Cie.*

## THE KNIGHT

From the cathedral of Reims.

The homeward-faring to receive.
No one's reports would they believe,
But only their own eyes' attest.
They found God's wonder manifest:
1395 A body healed, restored a life.
As for the peasant and his wife,
As one would well have known they might —
And who'd have robbed them of their right —
Ahead of all the rest they pressed.
1400 Their joy can never be expressed,
Nor the delight with which they fared;
For God in heaven had prepared
A joyous feast for loving eyes.
It brought the marvelous surprise
1405 Of master healed, of living child.
There never was a joy more wild
Than the parents now received,
When, once seeing, they believed
That both were sound and well in fact.
1410 They scarcely knew how they should act!
The greetings that they sought to say
Were broken in the strangest way:
So great a joy their bosoms swelled
That from their laughter great tears welled
1415 Within their eyes; they laughed, they cried.
The statement is not falsified:
Love for their child could not desist —
Three times and more her mouth they kissed.

The Swabians[26] received the knight
1420 With lovely gifts that pleased his sight;
Of their good will these were the token.
God knows, that if the truth is spoken
By those who've seen them, all must own,
No finer will is ever shown
1425 Than by the Swabians. And now, when
Thus greeted by his countrymen
Herr Heinrich came his homeward way,

What more still would you have me say
As to events that then transpired?
1430 Still greater riches he acquired
Than e'er, in goods and honored name.
But henceforth he applied the same
To serving God. He never swerved,
And God's commandments he observed
1435 Far better than he'd done before,
Thus honoring himself the more.

The peasant and his wife, the pair
Deserved that well they both should fare
In honors and material good.
1440 Nor was he of so fickle mood
As not most generous to requite.
He gave them land in their own right,
The field of which above we spoke —
The ground, and with it too, its folk,
1445 Where he when sick had gone to stay.
His spouse he served in every way.
He gave her goods, he gave her ease,
All sorts of presents bound to please.
No wife could more devotion own.
1450 It was a gratitude well shown!

Now the experienced and the wise
Began to urge and to advise
That he should marry; but, indeed,
Their counsel was not all agreed.
1455 He told them then his mind: He would,
In case they thought it well and good,
At once for kin and followers send,
And bring the matter to an end
According to their sentiment.[27]
1460 His summons now he ordered sent;
In all directions this occurred,
To all who heeded Heinrich's word.
When they had come together then,
Both kinsmen and his vassal men,

1465 To them he made the matter known.
They answered in a common tone,
'Twas right, and time, to take a wife.
But now arose a lively strife
Among the men who would advise —
1470 Their counsel was contrariwise,
Exactly as we usually find
When different people speak their mind.

Their views divergent as could be,
Poor Heinrich spoke now, thoughtfully.
1475 "As all who're gathered here well know,
I, but a little while ago
Was most unpleasant to behold,
Disgusting to my friends of old.
Now, neither men nor women flee.
1480 Our Lord's command, as you can see,
Has given me health in every limb.
Advise me, in the name of him
By whom this mercy has been shown,
The mercy which, I gladly own,
1485 Has made me well, as you discern:
How can I pay him back in turn?"

They said: "Resolve within yourself
That both your body and your wealth
Will always at his service stand."
1490 His dear young "spouse" stood close at hand.
Gently now he toward her faced,
And said, as he the girl embraced:
"You have already heard it said,
I owe it to this good young maid
1495 Whom you see standing by me here,
That I'm restored to health and cheer.
As I am, she is likewise free.[28]
My every thought now counsels me
To wed her; what do you advise?
1500 If it be proper in God's eyes,
I wish to ask her for her hand.

133

If that can't be, then understand
That I shall die without a wife;
For both my honor and my life
1505 Through her alone have been restored.
Now by the grace of our dear Lord,
I beseech you, if you can,
To give approval to my plan."

They all approved of Heinrich's choice.
1510 Both rich and poor said with one voice,
More fitly he could not have planned.
Enough of priests there were at hand:[29]
They gave her to him as his wife.
After a long and happy life,
1515 Each one inherited a place
Before the eternal throne of grace.
They went the path we all must go,
Whether it pleases us or no.
Heaven's reward, which each won then,
1520 God help us all to win. Amen!

# NOTES

# NOTES

## MEIER HELMBRECHT

[1] The title originates from the Ambras MS (A), which begins with the heading: *Das puech ist von dem Mayr Helmprechte*. It is not the peasant, however, but the peasant's son, who is the hero. The title *Meier* (from Lat. *major*), which originally meant the head servant or manager on a farm, came to be used later also for a tenant farmer.

[2] The poets of this period gained increased interest from their hearers by statements that their story was not invented, but true. Wernher's repeated assertions as to the truth of his story (cf. vss. 9, 16, 30 f., 73, 89, 208) would find sufficient explanation as a common stylistic device for heightening the interest. Cf. C. Schröder, "Heimat und Dichter des Helmbrecht," *Germ* X (1865), 456. Criticism is largely agreed, however, in accepting the *Helmbrecht* story as based upon actual occurrence. Cf. Introduction, pp. 9 ff., and *Der Arme Heinrich*, note 2.

[3] In the following description of the hood, the symbol of Helmbrecht's pride and fall, Wernher takes his departure from Neidhart (cf. below, vs. 217, and note 12), upon whom he elaborates, deriding the peasant's love of ostentatious dress, and perhaps burlesquing the pompous descriptions that prevailed in the court epics of his time. Popular poetry, however, has always loved such detailed description of works of art. The Homeric description of Achilles' shield may have served as a more remote model (*Iliad* 18, 483 ff.), and Virgil's descriptions of the pictures in the temple at Carthage (*Aeneid*, 8, 626 ff.). Tapestries, cloths and garments, to say nothing of saddles, shields, and the like, were covered with picture after picture, in almost every important poem of the middle ages. Embroidery, as everyone knows who is acquainted with the medieval arts, was the most artistic accomplishment of the period. Cf. McLaughlin, *Meier Helmbrecht*, p. 103. The hood is neither a nightcap nor a helmet. Helmbrecht himself tells us (303 ff.) that it is a headdress suitable for a knight. Such hoods were the fashion of the time, and only the over-ornateness of Helmbrecht's hood and the impropriety of a peasant's wearing the like were cause for attention. The hood is to be thought of as consisting of four sections or fields, divided by broad seam-bands. Silk-embroidered birds ornament only the surface of the seam-bands. On the fields between the bands were pictured legendary scenes. Cf. Braune, "Helmbrechts Haube," *Btr* XXXII (1907), 555 ff., and Meyer, "Helmbrecht und seine Haube," *ZfdPh* XL (1908), 421 ff.

[4] Middle High German *spehteshart* (= *Spechtswald*) means a forest where the woodpecker lives. Keinz and other commentators after him consider that the word is used here as a common noun and believe that it does not refer to the well-known mountain forest of this name lying far away in Middle Germany, southeast of Frankfurt am Main. W. Braune ("Helmbrechts Haube," *loc. cit.*, p. 556, note) takes issue with Keinz's view. The German Spessart was famous

in literature, and Braune believes that Wernher was familiar with it from its prominence in the epics of his time (*Nibelungenlied*; Wolfram's poems).

[5] The prominence which the legend of Troy held in the literature of Wernher's time is instanced by two poetic treatments which are still extant: Herbort von Fritzlar's epic, *Liet von Troye*, and Konrad von Würzburg's *Trojanischer Krieg*.

[6] The legend of Charlemagne was the subject for extensive epic treatment in Middle High German literature, as, for instance, in Pfaffe Konrad's *Rolandslied*. This epic was cast in a new version just in Wernher's time by the Austrian poet Der Stricker. The Frankish princes Turpin and Oliver were close followers of Charlemagne.

[7] Wilhelm ("Zur Abfassungszeit des Meier Helmbrecht," *Münchener Museum für Philol. des Mittelalters und der Renaissance*, III (1917-18), 226 ff.), regarding this line as reminiscent of the *Jüngere Titurel*, vss. 111 and 192, uses it to fix the date of the poem between the years 1270 and 1282. His argument, however, is conclusively refuted by Panzer ("Zum Meier Helmbrecht," *Btr* XLIX (1924), 150).

[8] The reference here is to the battle of Ravenna, in which Dietrich von Bern (Theodoric of Verona) and his East Goths defeated Odoacer in the year 493. The story of this event lives in the cycle of Middle High German epics that grew around the name of Dietrich. In the epic *Die Rabenschlacht* and in the folk-song *Strît vor Rabene*, Scharpf and Ort, the two sons of Etzel (Attila) and his wife Helche, are slain, together with Dietrich's younger brother Diether, by the hand of the notorious traitor Wittich.

[9] The clothing of the peasants had been prescribed by law since the time of Charlemagne. It consisted, according to the *Kaiserchronik*, of a coarse shirt, gray or black jacket with knee trousers to match, and leather shoes. The peasant was forbidden under severe penalty to wear a sword, a regulation which Friedrich I had renewed in 1156. Thus the equipment which Helmbrecht received from his mother and sister, including a linen shirt, a coat of mail and a sword, was such as a peasant's son was not qualified to wear.

[10] For the importance of these place names in identification of the scene of the action, see Introduction, pp. 9 f., and Keinz, *Helmbrecht und seine Heimat*, *passim*.

[11] The poet's description of this costume, although somewhat overdrawn, is in the main not a caricature. Buttons of the greatest possible variety of colors were in high favor. It was also the fashion to sew little bells upon the jacket, and even to fasten a bell upon each spur.

[12] Neidhart von Reuenthal, a Bavarian knight, stands foremost among the Middle High German writers of village poetry. In contrast to the court minnesingers, he occupied himself in his songs with village lads and lasses. Cf. Introduction, pp. 11 ff.

[13] Helmbrecht senior was not a serf, but a free man. He had to pay in produce an annual tenth, as farm rental, to his overlord, possibly to the monastery at Ranshofen. Cf. Introduction, p. 13.

[14] While the poorer classes wore coarse leather shoes, the finer shoes of the wealthy were made of a leather called *Corduan*, which doubtless derived its name from the fact that the knowledge of how to prepare fine leather came from Cordova.

<sup>15</sup> Such cloth was not kept in rolls by the peasants, but in folds (M. H. G. *sturz*) of one and a half to two feet, one over the other.

<sup>16</sup> "Ten pounds" (of pennies). The peasant of this period accomplished purchase or sale more commonly by exchange than by means of money. Compare the payment of the nun for the embroidering of the hood (vss. 119 ff.). It is a period of transition from barter to money exchange. The coins were of such small denominations that they were weighed rather than counted — a practice which was also desirable because of debased coinage and because of the lack of standard mintage. Two hundred and forty pennies make a pound. Cf. Keinz, *Helmbrecht und seine Heimat*, p. 81, note to vs. 399; Hagelstange, *Süddeutsches Bauernleben im Mittelalter*, pp. 126 f.

<sup>17</sup> For the significance of this passage in determining the date of the poem, see Introduction, p. 19.

<sup>18</sup> The expression "a wild Saxon" is proverbial in Middle High German literature. From the time of their forced conversion to Christianity by Charlemagne, the Low Saxons living in Westphalia and northward to the sea were considered to be a particularly wild people. Ernst Martin (*Gudrun*, Halle, 1872, note to st. 366, vs. 4) furnishes a list of allusions to Saxon wildness.

<sup>19</sup> This prophesy receives further explanation by the father's first dream, told in verses 580 ff.

<sup>20</sup> The inference from this and subsequent passages (vss. 783, 1606) that fish was regarded in South German territory as a particularly fine, aristocratic dish, finds direct substantiation in Seifried Helbling (VIII, vss. 884 ff.), who states that fish was a food for lords and was not a peasant article of diet. The epic *Der Ring*, much later in date, is similarly explicit:

> Du retst umb visch? Du bist nicht weis.
> Wis, es ist ein herren speis.

Hügli, *Der deutsche Bauer im Mittelalter*, p. 129, note 96, says with reference to the peasant in medieval German literature: *Weintrinkende und Fische essende Bauern sind immer unerhört freche Protzen.* Cf. Schiffmann, "Studien zum Helmbrecht," *Btr* XLII (1917), 6 f.; Hagelstange, *Süddeutsches Bauernleben*, p. 119; Schultz, *Das höfische Leben zur Zeit der Minnesänger*, I, 287.

<sup>21</sup> The relationship of godfather to godchild was highly esteemed in the middle ages, and was placed on a level with blood relationship. The popular belief still lingers in portions of Germany that qualities — particularly moral characteristics — pass from the godfather to his godchild. Cf. Sprenger, "Zum Meier Helmbrecht," *Germ* XXXVII (1892), 414. This idea of heritage from the godparent is expressed again below, vss. 1374 ff.

<sup>22</sup> Gough ("The Authorship of . . . Meier Helmbrecht," *loc. cit.*, p. 65), according to whose view Wernher was a monk of the Franciscan Order, says of these lines: "We have [here] an utterance that is quite inexplicable, except when spoken by a follower of St. Francis, to whom the wolf, the bird, even fire itself, were Brother Wolf, Sister Bird, and Brother Fire." For discussion of the pride in occupation revealed in this speech, see Introduction, pp. 16, 18.

<sup>23</sup> Keinz considers it probable that one of the robber knights' strongholds situated on the lower Inn River is meant — perhaps Ratishof, the largest and most notorious of these castles. Keinz, *Helmbrecht und seine Heimat*, p. 83, note to vss. 654 f.

<sup>24</sup> As though they had never had a grief to bear. The peasant loved his

cattle and lived intimately with them. The loss of a calf troubled him as would the death of a child.

25 The messenger who brought good news received a reward. This was known as the *Botenbrot*. Cf. Hagelstange, *Süddeutsches Bauernleben*, p. 33.

26 Middle High German *kneht* (or *frîman*) and *frîwîp*. These servants were not serfs, but hired help. Cf. R. Schröder, "Corpus Juris Germanici Poeticum," *Zfd Ph* II (1870), 302 ff.

27 Helmbrecht seeks to express himself in as many different languages as possible to dazzle his home folk with evidence of his extensive travel and of his contact with the higher world. He first uses a mutilated form of Low German or Flemish, in which he says: "My dear sweet children, God bless you!" The use of Flemish phrases in one's speech was considered a special mark of polish, since the tongue was spoken in territory which lay nearest to the culture of Northern France. (C. Schröder, "Die höfische Dorfpoesie des deutschen Mittelalters," *Jahrbuch für Literaturgeschichte*, I (1865), 64. Cf. Neidhart, 82, 2: *Mit sîner rede er vlaemet.*) The Latin phrase *Gratia vester*, which he had picked up somewhere, is also incorrect for *Gratia vestra* (Your Grace). The greeting *Dieu vous salue* (God greet you) naturally stands in the original in Old French *Deu sal*; it is equivalent to the present-day greeting of South Germany *Grüss Gott. Dobré jitró* (Good day) is a Bohemian greeting. The Austrian poet Seifried Helbling complains of its use in Austria as an aping of Bohemian custom (cf. E. Schröder, review of Seemüller, "Studien zum kleinen Lucidarius," *AfdA* X (1884), 56 ff.). For an interesting discussion of Wernher's source for details of this home-coming scene, cf. Panzer, "Zum Meier Helmbrecht," *Btr* XXXIII (1908), 391 ff.

28 Here again Helmbrecht mangles the dialect which he attempts to speak. The original contains a mixture of Low and High German forms. "What did you, stupid peasant, say to me, and the confounded woman? Forsooth, on my horse and my handsome person no awkward peasant shall ever lay hands!"

29 Since the fingers were still used at table rather than a fork, the washing of the hands before and after eating was a necessity. Cf. vs. 861.

30 Beds were at that time usually prepared upon the floor. Whether the bed upon the large tile stove was for a short rest before dinner or for the night as well, is not clear from this passage, nor from vss. 1043 ff. Large tile stoves such as that referred to may still be found in peasant rooms of South Germany and Tyrol. The peasant who wishes to stretch out after his day's labor usually lies down on the stove bench, or sometimes on the board scaffolding built over the stove, which in Tyrol is called the *Ofenbrugg*, or *aufm Ofen*. Cf. Zingerle, review of Stöwer, *Das Kulturhistorische im Meier Helmbrecht*, *AfdA* XIX (1893), 298.

31 Dinners of from six to seven courses were not unusual in court circles of this time, and the elaborate dinner here described is sufficiently explained by the joyful event of the son's home-coming. Keinz (*Helmbrecht und seine Heimat*, p. 84, note to vs. 867) comments that in the Helmbrecht region to this day each meal is begun with sauerkraut. G. G. Coulton, in his *Medieval Village* (p. 314), calls attention to the fact that even on this festive occasion with all its extravagant cheer, there is no wine or beer to drink.

32 See Introduction, pp. 9 f.

33 The Middle High German epic *Herzog Ernst*, which originated about 1180 on the lower Rhine, was one of the most popular poems of the middle ages in

Germany. It is extant in many manuscript versions, and lived on also in the form of a chapbook. The hero is Ernst II, duke of Swabia, than whom there have been few lustier cutthroats.

[34] The eating of cake with common bread was considered an offense against good taste. The rules of etiquette of the time have been preserved in both prose and verse form, as in Tannhäuser's *Hofzucht*, in the Viennese *Tischzucht*, and in Tomasin von Zirklaere's *Welscher Gast*. The loosening of the belt at table, as well as the blowing of the foam from one's drinking mug, is specifically criticized in Tannhäuser's *Hofzucht* as a violation of court etiquette.

[35] Lemberslint and the following names of Helmbrecht's comrades have been retained in German form, both to preserve color and because their retention made possible a much greater degree of faithfulness to the original in numerous passages. These names, which are satirical in nature, have the following connotations:

| | |
|---|---|
| Lämmerslint | Lambswallower |
| Schluckdenwidder | Bolt-the-ram |
| Höllensack | Hell's bag |
| Rüttelschrein | Pry-the-chest |
| Mausdenkelch | Pinch-the-communion-cup  (Church-robber) |
| Kuhfrass | Cow-glutton |
| Wolfsgaum | Wolfjaws |
| Wolfsrüssel | Wolfgullet |
| Wolfsdarm | Wolfgut |
| Schlingdasgeu | Devour-the-land |

Gustav Freytag's surmise that these names were not all invented by the author has, however, been substantiated. The names *Lemberslint, Chufrezz* and *Slintzgaew* have been found recorded in old Austrian legal documents that date since 1269. Similar names are reported by Grotefend in an article, "Über imperativische Namensformen. Ein Beitrag zur Entstehungsgeschichte der Personennamen," in *Mitteilungen des Vereins für Geschichte und Altertumskunde* (Frankfurt a. M.), VII (1885), 369-370. Cf. also Müller, "Beiträge zur Geschichte der mhd. Litteratur in Österreich," *AfdA* (1887), 96 ff.; Zingerle, review of Stöwer, *Das Kulturhistorische*, p. 297 note; Seemüller, "Studien zum kleinen Lucidarius," pp. 639 f.

[36] For preservation of their valuables the peasants used little iron boxes, about two feet long and four to five inches wide and high, equipped with a firm lock. These safe-boxes were sometimes built into the house. Keinz reports that such boxes, now called *Isolt*, are still in use in the Helmbrecht region (*Helmbrecht und seine Heimat*, p. 86, note to vs. 1205; Hagelstange, *Süddeutsches Bauernleben*, pp. 114 f.).

[37] A name invented from the German word *Narr* (fool). Compare the proper name *Narragonien* in Sebastian Brant's *Narrenschiff*.

[38] This passage, which reads in the original:

diesen henk ich in die wide
bi den sparrâdern sin

has presented difficulty. The M. H. G. dictionaries fail to record a suitable definition of the word *sparrâder*; they carry as the meaning *Krampfader* (varicose vein), which is impossible in this context. In accord with Sprenger ("Zum Meier Helmbrecht," *loc. cit.*, p. 408), most translators have treated the word as

141

meaning *heel*. I have shown that the accurate meaning here is *sinew, tendon* (of Achilles). Bell, "Helmbrecht 1251," *Mod. Lang. Notes*, XXXIX (1924), 372 ff.

[39] According to old popular belief, the sheriff had the power by his fixed gaze to charm a criminal to the spot or to cause him to obey his every command. This superstition finds expression again in vss. 1625 f. and 1640 ff., and accounts for the swift action in vss. 1614 ff.

[40] Wernher's technique is crude here. Not until vss. 1431 f. do we learn that the father, vexed and deeply troubled, has turned away, so that the conversation which ensues between young Helmbrecht and his sister was out of earshot of the parents.

[41] Burial at crossroads was in former times the method of disposing of executed criminals and suicides.

[42] According to Keinz (*Helmbrecht und seine Heimat*, p. 87, note to vss. 1306 ff.) the custom still prevails in some rural regions of South German territory, of carrying a pan of smoking embers around the corpse lying in the house. This is a survival of heathen custom, the purpose of which was to keep evil spirits from the dead. As for the period of a year's mourning mentioned, this is still observed almost everywhere by a surviving husband or wife.

[43] Cf. note 21.

[44] Bowing toward the direction in which one's beloved lived was, according to Bartsch, a court custom of Provençal origin. Cf. Lambel, *Meier Helmbrecht*, note to vs. 1461.

[45] A conventional expression, originating from the fact that at the medieval wedding celebration the bridal couple were given special seats of honor. The bridal chair is referred to in various epics as highly decorated (*Kudrun*, st. 549; *Athis C\**, vs. 7; *Erec*, vs. 7662) and is likened to a throne (*J. Titurel*, vs. 1505). Cf. Schultz, *Das höfische Leben*, I, 492.

[46] It was Hartmann von Aue who first introduced Arthurian legend into German literature. Arthur figures as one of the most resplendent knightly characters in the Middle High German epic.

[47] These verses impress one as a parody of the famous lines in Gottfried's *Tristan*:

> ein man, ein wip, ein wip, ein man —
> Tristan, Isolt, Isolt, Tristan.

Cf. Meyer, "Helmbrecht und seine Haube," *loc. cit.*, p. 426.

[48] We have here an interesting description of the early German marriage, which was a lay ceremony. It was the old heathen German custom to require the couple to enter a circle formed by those present. Some layman then questioned man and woman in turn. The Church, as early as the eighth century, began her attempts to bring weddings under her jurisdiction, but gained ground only slowly. The early German epics, and in particular the popular or folk epics, contain many illustrations of profane weddings, as well as weddings in connection with which church consecration took place only after the union had been consummated. In general it may be said that the higher classes bowed first to the church requirement, while among the lower classes the Gretna Green type of marriage persisted even into the fifteenth century. Cf. Grimm, *Deutsche Rechtsaltertümer*, p. 600, *sub voce* "kirchliche trauung"; Schultz, *Das höfische Leben*, I, 486; Wackernagel, "Verlöbnis und Trauung," *ZfdA* II (1842), 548-555; Hagelstange, *Süddeutsches Bauernleben*, p. 61; Friedberg, *Verlobung und Trau-*

*ung* (Leipzig, 1876), *passim*; and R. Sohm, *Trauung und Verlobung* (Weimar, 1876), *passim*.

49 This old custom was symbolic of taking possession. The superstition is said still to linger in this region that the one who first steps upon the other's foot at the wedding will have the upper hand. Keinz, *Helmbrecht und seine Heimat*, p. 90, note to vs. 1534. Cf. Grimm, *Deutsche Rechtsaltertümer*, I, 142, *sub voce* "Füsse."

50 The following description of the banquet is one of humorous irony. The various offices, such as marshal, cupbearer, steward and chamberlain, were known only at great court festivities. Cf. *Nibelungenlied*, stanzas 10, 11; and *Parzival* (ed. Bartsch), vss. 666, 1195 ff.

51 This is a very old popular superstition. The Germans still say of one who eats hastily and greedily: "Der Tod isst mit ihm." Cf. Lambel, *Meier Helmbrecht*, note to vss. 1568 ff.

52 When a thief was caught in the act or with the goods in his possession, such goods were tied upon his back and he was at once brought before the court, where judgment was spoken and carried out without defense. Cf. *Schwabenspiegel*, ch. 316; Grimm, *Deutsche Rechtsaltertümer*, pp. 637 ff.; Klibansky, "Gerichtsszene und Prozessform in erzählenden deutschen Dichtungen," *Germanische Studien*, XL (1925), 58.

53 The old German laws (cf. *Sachsenspiegel*, II, 31, par. 2) conceded to the judge the right to retain the stolen goods left by an executed person, if these were not demanded by the owner within a year.

54 The right of the hangman over the life of the tenth criminal is confirmed in the old German codes of law, *Sachsenspiegel* and *Schwabenspiegel*. Cf. R. Schröder, "Corpus Juris," pp. 303 ff.; Klibansky, "Gerichtsszene und Prozessform," *Germ. Studien*, XL (1925), 58 f. Haupt ("Kleine Bemerkungen, 2, Helmbrecht 1679 ff., *ZfdA* IV (1844), 579), cites a similar sparing of the tenth criminal at the siege of robbers in the castle of Schwanau by citizens of Strassburg in 1333. That in our poem the sheriff does not exercise his right to let the tenth criminal go entirely free, but inflicts drastic punishment, may be explained by the fact that there was no one who would pay him ransom money for Helmbrecht's liberation. For a discussion of the sheriff (M. H. G. *scherge*) and the importance of the title of this officer in determining the scene of the epic, cf. Schiffmann, "Studien zum Helmbrecht," p. 5; Panzer, "Zum Meier Helmbrecht," p. 148; and Klibansky, "Gerichtsszene und Prozessform," pp. 57 ff.

55 The right hand, the left foot. Cf. Grimm, *Deutsche Rechtsaltertümer*, pp. 705 ff.

56 The heathen German belief that the earth was made of the flesh of a god and was possessed of divine strength gave rise to various symbolical rites and superstitious practices. Wackernagel ("Erde der Leib Christi," *ZfdA* VI (1848), 288-289) states that the custom on the part of men facing a quick death by execution, by murder or in battle, of seizing a piece of earth and eating it, was a heathen practice. He presents passages from French, Italian and German epics, which show that the custom prevailed in French and Italian as well as in German territory. J. Grimm (*Deutsche Mythologie*, 4. Ausg. (1875), I, 534 ff.) states that German soldiers of the sixteenth century still retained the custom of casting a piece of earth before entrance into battle, as a sign of renunciation of life. Zingerle (*Sagen aus Tirol*, 2. Aufl. (1891), p. 464) shows the existence of a superstition that a witch who could gain possession of a piece of earth could

instantly break her bonds. It is apparent that as Christianity spread in the middle ages, the clergy supplied a Christian basis to the old popular superstitions. The earth came under their influence to be regarded as a symbol for Christ's body. Hence it was believed that a person dying without a spiritual consoler might use a piece of earth as a substitute for the sacred wafer in an emergency sacrament. Cf. Lambel, *Meier Helmbrecht*, p. 189, note to vs. 1905; Hagelstange, *Süddeutsches Bauernleben*, pp. 216 f.

## DER ARME HEINRICH

[1] The ability to read and especially to write was rare among medieval knights, and was sometimes not possessed even by poets of the Middle High German period. The knight depended upon a menial for such services when they were needed.

[2] This statement may be the stylistic device commonly used by the poets of the time to lend the weight of authority to their own inventions. More probably, however, it is an indication of Hartmann's use of a Latin source. Cf. Introduction, pp. 25 ff., and *Meier Helmbrecht*, note 2.

[3] Custom required this accomplishment of a knight. It was considered a sign of culture to write love lyrics, which were called *minnesongs*.

[4] Cf. Job 19. 9; Is. 28. 3; Lam. 5. 16. The language of *Der arme Heinrich* is overladen with metaphors, drawn mostly from the Bible or from church authors. Cf. Schönbach, *Über Hartmann von Aue*, pp. 130-155, 191. Ehrismann, *Geschichte der deutschen Literatur*, p. 202, note 4.

[5] Hartmann is in error here. The passage which he quotes does not occur in the Bible, but in a hymn composed by Notker the Stammerer, a monk of St. Gall, who died in the year 912: *Media vita in morte sumus; quem quaerimus adjutorem, nisi te, domine?*

[6] This is a biblical metaphor. Cf. Is. 28. 1, 4: "the fading flower of his glorious beauty."

[7] The home of leprosy seems to have been Egypt. Evidence shows the existence of the disease in Europe as early as the sixth century. It was probably introduced by the Romans from their provinces. The migrations of peoples, including the Jews, and the crusades were great spreading agents. Until the close of the middle ages the disease raged with virulence throughout Europe. Cf. Ehrismann, *Geschichte der deutschen Literatur*, p. 198.

[8] Montpellier ($<$ *mons pessulanus*) finds first mention as a medical school in 1137, and rose into prominence in the latter half of that century.

[9] A dramatic heightening. Salerno was the older and still more renowned school for doctors. Its fame extends back as far as the tenth century, and references to it are to be found throughout medieval literature. When Heinrich goes to Salerno, after his failure to find aid at Montpellier, he is taking recourse to the very highest source of medical authority.

[10] Bitterly ironical.

[11] Belief in the healing power of human blood — the fountain of life in the body — in cases of leprosy is as old as the disease itself. The blood of children, of young girls or of virgins was believed to be particularly effective; for the purer the means (through the innocence or holiness of the source from which drawn), the greater the efficacy was believed to be.

[12] The peasant rented his land from Heinrich. (It does not become his own

144

until vs. 1442.) His status as freeborn (*ein frîer bûman*) is of importance for the sequel of the narrative (vss. 1497 ff.). Cf. Schönbach, *Über Hartmann von Aue*, p. 309.

13 Beside the regular rentals, the feudal lord levied special assessments and exacted arbitrary services from time to time. Cf. Hügli, *Der Deutsche Bauer im Mittelalter*, p. 67, note 84.

14 "They say." Affirmation by reference to the authority of the legend. Cf. note 2, above.

15 This maiden, the heroine of the story, is nowhere named. Her youthful age has caused comment; she is, according to MS A, a child of only eight years; in B, however, she is twelve, and B may here be truer to the original. The lapse of the three years indicated in verse 351 make her but eleven (or fifteen) years old at the time of her marriage. One must, however, bear in mind the earlier ripeness of the women of the middle ages. The child already calls herself a maid (vs. 561), and she thinks of her single state as lasting at the most some two or three years more (vs. 748), when she would be thirteen (seventeen) years old. Medieval German laws recognized girls of twelve and boys of fourteen as marriageable. The Middle High German epics contain many allusions to similarly early marriages. Cf. Weinhold, *Die deutschen Frauen in dem Mittelalter*, 2. Aufl., I, 294.

16 Our numbering of verses follows Gierach, who in turn follows Haupt. In a few places it has proved difficult to retain in the translation the number of verses exactly as in the original. Thus discrepancies occur between verses 310 and 315, 330 and 335, 360 and 365, and 455 and 460. Where in his restored text Gierach inserts verses taken from versions not used by Haupt, he indicates the insertions by lettering the verses, as verses 652*a-d*, 654*a-b*, 662*a-d*, 852*a-b* and 980*a-b*.

17 God appears as gatekeeper in various church writings. The metaphor, suggested perhaps by John 10. 9: "I am the door," is a favorite one with medieval poets.

18 For explanation of the appellation "spouse," see verse 341.

19 Honor, according to Schönbach, *Über Hartmann von Aue* (p. 310), is to be interpreted here as consisting of one's rights and dignities within one's class which are not infringed upon by the *seigneur*.

20 The pronounced religious and didactic tone of the following extended speech reflects the monastic element in Hartmann's education, and perhaps to some extent the monkish original which he may have used as the basis of his poem. For interpretation of its psychology, see Introduction, pp. 27 f.

21 John 15. 1 represents Christ as a husbandman. The Church as the bride of Christ is likewise a metaphor familiar from the Bible. The concept of him as the bridegroom of the individual comes from the life of the convent, the inmates of which dedicated themselves to the heavenly Bridegroom. Entrance into the convent was considered the nun's betrothal, and death her marriage.

22 According to legend, St. Nicholas, while still in the cradle, abstained in fast from his mother's breast two days of the week.

23 The reference is to Luke 6. 23, 35. Cf. Matt. 5. 12; Luke 6. 23; also Rom. 2. 6.

24 Hartmann wrote *Cordis Speculator*, misquoting from the *Wisdom of Solomon*, 1. 6: "For God is . . . a true beholder (*scrutator*) of the heart."

[25] It was the medieval custom to give escort to the departing one for three days on his journey, and to go equally far to meet one returning home.

[26] This passage in praise of the Swabians is interpreted as evidence of Hartmann's Swabian origin.

[27] The approval of his kin was necessary for the marriage. Cf. Schönbach, *Über Hartmann von Aue*, pp. 313 ff.

[28] We are expressly told that the girl, although of peasant birth, was free (vs. 269). Heinrich, however, was of noble descent, and in the eyes of the prevailing medieval German law the free status of the girl did not prevent the marriage from being a *mésalliance*. The children of such a union followed the mother; they were not of the father's class, nor could they be his heirs. Kraut's *Privatrecht*, par. 57, however, records legal deviations of a milder nature, and Heinrich's marriage to the peasant girl indicates the probability that such deviations from the strict legal rule were possible. Wackernagel, *Der arme Heinrich* (reprint, 1885), p. 160, note. Such marriages are represented as common in the French literature of the preceding period — for example, the little story commonly translated as "The Divided Horse Cloth," which is to be found in the "Everyman's Series," in the *Aucassin* volume. Cf. Hügli, *Der deutsche Bauer im Mittelalter*, p. 68: "Die Ehe des adligen Grafen mit der Meierstochter ist so auch rechtlich gar nicht ausgeschlossen, denn durch den Landbesitz wird der vorher freie Lâze ein Vollfreier und steht nun rechtlich auch höher als der dienstadelige Ritter."

[29] As a matter of course in an epic showing so strong a monkish influence, we find here a church betrothal, in contrast to the lay wedding described a half century later in *Meier Helmbrecht*. Cf. note 48 to *Meier Helmbrecht*; Ehrismann, *Geschichte der deutschen Literatur*, p. 202, note 4.

# APPENDIX

# APPENDIX

The more serious student of *Meier Helmbrecht* inevitably feels an impulse to glean systematically from the text of the epic the many items of cultural information which it contains. This task has been frequently essayed. For English readers, the most accessible (although somewhat careless) treatment is that by Haertel.[1] In German, there are the studies by Inowraclawer,[2] Stöwer,[3] Hagelstange[4] and Hügli.[5] The wealth of concrete detail which Wernher affords us will be sufficiently illustrated here by a study of a single phase of life as pictured in the poem: food.

The peasant's life in Helmbrecht's time was closely circumscribed by sumptuary laws.[6] These permitted him to eat kraut, oat or barley soup and meat — during fast-periods hemp, lentils and beans — while wild game, fish and oil are forbidden. These regulations are given in Seifried Helbling,[7] together with a complaint that the peasants so little observe them. The foods first mentioned in our poem are beef, cheese and eggs, given to the nun who embroidered Helmbrecht's hood.[8] Cheese and eggs are also carried to court by the peasants.[9] The staple article of food on the peasant's table is a soup or porridge.[10] The poor mixed this porridge with water instead of milk.[11] The father urges his son to content himself with this dish, mixing a bit of rye with his oats, rather than to demand chicken,[12] goose[13] and ill-gotten fish.[14] Fish is several times referred to in a way which indicates that it was

---

[1] "Social Conditions in Southern Bavaria," *op. cit.*    [2] *Meier Helmbrecht.*
[3] *Das Kulturhistorische im Meier Helmbrecht.*
[4] *Süddeutsches Bauernleben im Mittelalter.*
[5] *Der deutsche Bauer im Mittelalter.*
[6] *Leopoldinischer Landfrieden* (Herzog Leopold VI, der Glorreiche). Cf. Hügli, *op. cit.*, p. 81.    [7] VIII, vss. 874 ff.    [8] Vss. 119, 125 ff.    [9] Vs. 917.
[10] Vss. 454 ff.    [11] Vss. 1240 f.    [12] Vs. 452.    [13] Vs. 457.    [14] Vs. 464.

an aristocratic dish that was not served on a peasant's table.[15]
The "meal-cake" mentioned in vss. 445 f., which the father
holds up as a food fit for a nobleman, is in the original termed
*clamirre*; some think it was a sort of sandwich, made of baked
slices of rolls or buns interlaid with brain or with fruit. The
peasant eats black bread, made possibly of oats and rye;[16]
white bread is eaten by the nobles.[17] *Gîselitze* is a dish familiar
to the Helmbrecht table;[18] the term is translatable into modern
German as *Grütze* (groats). That meat was comparatively
rare upon the peasant's table may be inferred from passages
such as 1122 and 1291. But since cattle, hogs, sheep,[19] goats,[20]
chickens[21] and geese[22] were raised, a variety of meat and
fowl, as well as milk and eggs, must have been available.
Cabbage[23] and beets or turnips[24] are the only vegetables mentioned. By way of cake, verse 1143 mentions *krâpfen*, which
seem to have been something like crullers. Wernher empha-
sizes by repeated reference that wine, mead and beer are never
drunk by the peasant. The latter contents himself with water
and urges his son to be likewise content with this good drink
from the home well.[25] Even upon the joyous occasion of the
son's first return home, when an elaborate course dinner was
served, there was only fresh spring water to drink.[26] Young
Helmbrecht avers that an obnoxious rich peasant drank beer,[27]
and boasts that he will avenge the latter's breach of manners
in blowing the foam from his mug. The knights, on the other
hand, revel and carouse in the beverages that are so strikingly
absent from Meier Helmbrecht's board.[28]

Two gala dinners are described in the course of the poem:
the first, served by the peasant family to the homecoming
"knight";[29] the second, the wedding banquet served in honor
of Lämmerslint and Gotelint.[30] Concerning the latter we are
told only in a general way that there was a lavish abundance
of meats roast and boiled,[31] of fish,[32] bread[33] and wine.[34] The

---

[15] Vss. 783, 1606. Cf. note to *Meier Helmbrecht*, No. 20.     [16] Vss. 461, 479.
[17] Vs. 478.     [18] Vs. 473.     [19] Vs. 282.     [20] Vs. 674.     [21] Vss. 126, 172, 881, 917.
[22] Vs. 874.     [23] Vss. 867, 1604.     [24] Vs. 1361.
[25] Vss. 443 f., 471 f., 793 f., 891 ff.     [26] Vs. 891 ff.     [27] Vs. 1166.
[28] Vss. 794, 985 ff., 1401, 1541, 1555.     [29] Vss. 860 ff.     [30] Vss. 1470 ff., 1535 ff.
[31] Vs. 1549.     [32] Vs. 1606.     [33] Vs. 1550.     [34] Vs. 1555.

dinner of welcome to the returned son is described in greater detail, even to the naming of the most important courses.

Before sitting down to eat, Helmbrecht washes his hands;[35] the fork, as an eating utensil, is still unknown. The first course served to him is a fine-cut sauerkraut.[36] Meat, both fat and lean, came with this dish; it is not clear from the text whether it had been packed away with the sauerkraut or was served as an accompanying dish. Next, a ripe, mellow cheese is served,[37] followed by a large goose which had been roasted on a spit.[38] Two chickens, one boiled, one roasted, are then brought on the table.[39] However abstemious the peasant of this period commonly was, he could upon occasion be a hearty eater; the rules of etiquette of the time forbade the loosening of one's belt at table.[40] Many other dishes are mentioned as having been served at this dinner, although they are not specifically named,[41] and the father says: "If I had wine, we'd drink it now, dear son. Drink instead the best spring water that ever flowed from the earth!" [42] Yet after a week or so of the plain home fare following the welcoming banquet, Helmbrecht buckles his belt three holes tighter from lack of wine and meat, and feels that he must break away to enjoy his wonted carousings.

---

[35] Vs. 861.  [36] Vs. 867.  [37] Vs. 871.  [38] Vs. 874.
[39] Vs. 881.  [40] Vs. 1152.  [41] Vss. 887 f.  [42] Vss. 891 ff.

# BIBLIOGRAPHY

## ABBREVIATIONS FOR PERIODICALS MOST FREQUENTLY REFERRED TO

*AfdA*   *Anzeiger für deutsches Altertum und deutsche Literatur* (bound with *ZfdA*)

*Btr*   *Beiträge zur Geschichte der deutschen Sprache und Literatur*

*DLZ*   *Deutsche Literaturzeitung*

*Germ*   *Germania*

*JbPh*   *Jahresberichte über die Erscheinungen auf dem Gebiete der germanischen Philologie*

*JEGPh*   *Journal of English and Germanic Philology*

*Lbl*   *Literaturblatt für germanische und romanische Philologie*

*LCbl*   *Literarisches Centralblatt*

*RC*   *Revue critique d'histoire et de littératur*

*ZfdA*   *Zeitschrift für deutsches Altertum und deutsche Literatur*

*ZfdPh*   *Zeitschrift für deutsche Philologie*

*ZföGy*   *Zeitschrift für österreichische Gymnasien*

# BIBLIOGRAPHY

The arrangement in the Bibliography is chronological: Names of authors and editors will be found in alphabetical order in the Index.

## I. MEIER HELMBRECHT

### Manuscripts

MS B (Berlin MS). *Hie hebt sich ain mår von dem Helmprecht der was ain nar und auch ain gauglår amen.* Austria, 15th century. Manuscripta Germanica folio 470 in the Preussische Staatsbibliothek, pp. 229*b* to end.

MS A (Ambras MS). *Das puech ist von dem Mayr Helmprechte.* In Ambraser Heldenbuch, Wien, *ca.* 1510, pp. 225*b*-229*b*. The Heldenbuch was recorded by Hans Ried, 1504-1515, at command of Kaiser Maximilian. The more reliable of the two MSS.

### Middle High German Editions

*Von dem Mayr Helmprechte* . . . hrsg. von J. Bergmann. Wien, 1839. *Wiener Jahrbücher der Literatur*, Anzeigeblatt zu Bd. LXXXV und LXXXVI. Printed separately, Wien, 1839. A print of MS A.

> Reviewed: Anon., *Göttingische gelehrte Anzeigen* (1839), III, 1740-1743.

*Helmbrecht*, hrsg. von M. Haupt. *ZfdA* IV (1844), 318-385. Critical edition.

*Helmbrecht, von Wernher dem Gartener*, hrsg. von F. H. von der Hagen. Stuttgart, Tübingen, 1850. *Gesammtabenteuer*, Bd. III, Nr. 66, pp. 271-335. Based on MS B.

*Meier Helmbrecht*, hrsg. von Karl Goedeke. *Deutsche Dichtung im Mittelalter.* Hannover, 1854, pp. 826-840; 2. Aufl., Dresden, 1871. Based on Haupt's text.

*Helmbrecht und seine Heimat*, von Friedrich Keinz. München, 1865; 2. Aufl., Leipzig, 1887. *Nachträge, Sitzungsberichte der königl. bayer. Akademie der Wissenschaften zu München*, Philosophisch-philologische Classe, I (1865), 316-331. Based on Haupt's text.

REVIEWED: Edw. Schröder, *DLZ* VIII (1887), 1271; Anon., *JbPh* IX (1887), 162-163; Kinzel, *ZfdPh* XX (1888), 379; Anon., *LCbl* XLVIII (1887), 1633; Lambel, *Lbl* XIII (1892), 369-374.

*Meier Helmbrecht, von Wernher dem Gärtner*, hrsg. von H. Lambel. In *Erzählungen und Schwänke*. Leipzig, 1872, pp. 123-190; 2. Aufl., 1883, pp. 131 ff. *Deutsche Klassiker des Mittelalters*, hrsg. von Pfeiffer. Bd. XII. Based on Haupt's text.

*Wernher der Gärtner*, hrsg. von P. Piper. Stuttgart, 1889. *Kürschners Deutsche Nationalliteratur*, Bd. IV, Teil 2, Höfische Epik, 2, pp. 398 ff. Based on Haupt's text.

*Meier Helmbrecht, von Wernher dem Gartenaere*, hrsg. von Friedrich Panzer. Halle, 1902; 4. Aufl., 1924. *Altdeutsche Textbibliothek*, hrsg. von H. Paul. Nr. 11. Critical edition. Most widely used text.

REVIEWED: αλι, *LCbl* LIII (1902), 1403-1404; Schönbach, *Österreichisches Litteraturblatt*, XI, 687; Ehrismann, *ZfdPh* XXXVI (1904), 275-277; Lambel, *AfdA* XXIX (1904), 214-227.

*Wernher der Gärtner, Meier Helmbrecht*. Für die Schule bearbeitet von Johann Pilz. Wien, 1924.

*Wernher der Gartenaere: Meier Helmbrecht*. Hrsg. und erklärt von Dr. Hans Fluck. Paderborn [1926]. *Ferdinand Schöninghs Dombücherei*, Heft 22.

MODERN GERMAN METRICAL TRANSLATIONS

*Meier Helmbrecht, von Wernher dem Gärtner*. Die älteste deutsche Dorfgeschichte, übertragen von Carl Schröder. Wien, 1865; 2. Aufl., Troppau [no date].

*Meier Helmbrecht, von Wernher dem Gärtner*. Die älteste deutsche Dorfgeschichte . . . übersetzt von Karl Pannier. Cöthen, 1876.

*Meier Helmbrecht, von Wernher dem Gärtner*. Die älteste deutsche Dorfgeschichte . . . mit Einleitung und Erläuterung von Max Oberbreier. Leipzig, 1878. Reclam, Nr. 1188.

*Drei Erzählungen aus dem deutschen Mittelalter*, übersetzt von Gotthold Klee. Stuttgart, 1889. *Deutsche Jugend- und Volksbibliothek*, Nr. 124. Pages 89-121: *Junker Helmbrecht der Bauernsohn*.

*Meier Helmbrecht, von Wernher dem Gärtner* . . . Nach C. Schröders Textübersetzung. Für Schule und Haus hrsg. von Wohlrabe. Leipzig, 1883; 4. Aufl., 1914. Expurgated edition of Schröder's translation.

*Meier Helmbrecht, von Wernher dem Gärtner* . . . Eine deutsche Novelle aus dem 13. Jh. Übersetzt von Ludwig Fulda. Berlin, Leipzig [1889]. *Bibliothek der Gesamtliteratur,* Nr. 289. [Neudruck] Berlin, 1924. *Hendel-Bücher,* Nr. 289.

REVIEWED: Elias, *AfdA* XV (1889), 213; Anon., *JbPh* XI (1889), 202; Lambel, *Lbl* XIII (1892), 369-374; Sprenger, *ZfdPh* XXIV (1892), 132-133.

*Meier Helmbrecht, von Wernher dem Gärtner* . . . übersetzt und erläutert von Gotthold Bötticher. Halle, 1891. *Denkmäler der älteren deutschen Literatur,* hrsg. von G. Bötticher und K. Kinzel, Bd. II, 69 ff.

REVIEWED: Lambel, *Lbl* XIII (1892), 369-374; Erdmann, *ZfdPh* XXIV (1892), 139-140.

*Helmbrecht.* Ein oberösterreichisches Gedicht aus dem 13. Jh. von Wernher dem Gärtner, übertragen von Konrad Schiffmann. Linz, 1905.

REVIEWED: Bernt, *ZföGy* LVI (1905), 742-744.

*Meier Helmbrecht, von Wernher dem Gärtner* . . . Neudeutsch von Will Vesper. München, 1906. *Statuen deutscher Kultur,* hrsg. von Will Vesper, Bd. VIII. Neuausgabe, München, 1921.

*Meier Helmbrecht, von Wernher dem Gärtner,* übertragen von Fritz Bergemann. Leipzig [1920]. *Inselbücherei,* Nr. 304.

REVIEWED: E. Schröder, *AfdA* XL (1921), 149.

*Wernher der Gärtner: Meier Helmbrecht.* Neu übertragen und hrsg. von Johannes Seiler. Bielefeld, 1921. Velhagen und Klasings *Sammlung deutscher Schulausgaben,* Bd. 80.

*Wernher der Gartenaere, Meier Helmbrecht,* in neuhochdeutscher Nachdichtung, von Johann Pilz. Wien, 1923. Mit Bildbeigaben von Maximilian Liebenwein. *Deutsche Hausbücherei,* Bd. 95.

*Prachtausgabe des Meier Helmbrechts von Wernher dem Gartenaere.* Mittelhochdeutsch und Neuhochdeutsch in Gegenüberstellung. Mit 80 grösstenteils farbigen Voll- und Rahmenbildern in Steindruck nach Originalen von Maximilian Liebenwein. Amalthea Verlag, Zürich, Leipzig, Wien, 1923.

*Werner der Gärtner: Meier Helmbrecht.* Von Karl Schiffmann aus dem Mittelhochdeutschen ins Hochdeutsche übertragen, mit 12 Holzschnitten von Herm. Dienz. Leipzig, Zürich, Wien, 1924.

*Meier Helmbrecht, von Wernher dem Gärtner.* Versnovelle aus der Zeit des niedergehenden Rittertums, in neuem Reime dargeboten von Johannes Ninck. Leipzig [1927]. Reclam, Nr. 1188.

## MODERN GERMAN PROSE VERSIONS

*Der Bauernsohn Helmbrecht.* Nach einer altdeutschen Novelle Wernhers des Gärtners. Mit Illustrationen von Albert Zeh und August Gaber. Dresden, 1863. Programm.

*Aus deutschen Dörfern.* In *Bilder aus der deutschen Vergangenheit,* von Gustav Freytag. Leipzig, 1859-1867. Bd. II, Abt. 2, pp. 51 ff.

*Helmbrecht.* Eine Bauerngeschichte aus dem 13. Jh., Wernher dem Gärtner nacherzählt von Paul Wüst. Wiesbaden, 1911. *Wiesbadener Volksbücher,* Nr. 148.

*Meier Helmbrecht.* Eine österreichische Dorfgeschichte aus dem 13. Jh. Erzählt von Karl Linke. [Farb.] Bilder von W. Dachauer. Wien, 1924.

*Der Meier Helmbrecht,* Wernher dem Gartenaere nacherzählt, von Josef Hofmiller. München, 1925.

## DRAMATIZATIONS

*Meier Helmbrecht.* Schauspiel in einem Akt, von Karl Felner. Berlin, Leipzig, 1906.

*Meier Helmbrecht.* Volksdrama in fünf Akten, von Ernst Ege. Stuttgart, 1906.

REVIEWED: Goes, "Helmbrecht: Eine alte Novelle und ein neues Drama." *Christliche Welt,* XXI (1907), 699-704.

*Meier Helmbrecht.* Eine Tragödie in einem Vorspiel und drei Akten, von Eugen Ortner. München, 1928.

## ENGLISH PROSE VERSION

*Meier Helmbrecht, a German Farmer of the Thirteenth Century,* by Edward Tompkins McLaughlin. In *Studies in Medieval Life and Literature.* New York, London, 1894, pp. 100-122. A recapitulation, with occasional passages in prose translation.

## CRITICAL LITERATURE

Haupt, M., "Kleine Bemerkungen, 2, Meier Helmbrecht." *ZfdA* III (1843), 279.

Haupt, M., "Kleine Bemerkungen, 2, Helmbrecht 1679 ff."
*ZfdA* IV (1844), 579.

Haupt, M., "Zu Helmbrecht 422." *ZfdA* V (1845), 471.

Pfeiffer, Franz, "Zum Helmbrecht." *ZfdA* V (1845), 471.

Pfeiffer, Franz, "Forschung und Kritik auf dem Gebiete des deutschen Altertums, I, Über Meier Helmbrecht." *Sitzungsberichte der philosophisch-historischen Classe der kaiserlichen Akademie der Wissenschaften*, Wien, XLI (1863), 288-312.

Hoffmann, C., "Über den Meier Helmbrecht." (Mit einem Kärtchen.) *Sitzungsberichte der königl. bayer. Akademie der Wissenschaften*, Philosophisch-philologische Classe, München, II (1864), 181-191.

Hoffmann, C., "Nachträge des Herrn Keinz zum Meier Helmbrecht." *Sitzungsberichte der königl. bayer. Akademie der Wissenschaften*, Philosophisch-philologische Classe, München, I (1865), 316-331.

Schröder, Carl, "Heimat und Dichter des Helmbrecht." *Germ* X (1865), 455-464.

Keinz, Fr., *Zur Helmbrecht-Kritik in Pfeiffers "Germania."* München, 1866.

Meyer, K., *Untersuchungen über das Leben Reinmars von Zweter und Bruder Wernhers.* Basel, 1866.

Jänicke, Oskar, "Kleinere Bemerkungen, Helmbrecht 1388." *ZfdA* XIV (1869), 558-559.

Schröder, C., "Bruder Wernher und der Dichter des Meier Helmbrecht." *Ergänzungsblätter zur Kenntnis der Gegenwart*, III (1869), 724.

Schröder, Richard, "Corpus Juris Germanici Poeticum, II, Wernher der Gartenaere und Bruder Wernher." *ZfdPh* II (1870), 302-305.

Birlinger, A., "Zu Meier Helmbrecht." *Germ* XVI (1871) 82.

Birlinger, A., "Zum Meier Helmbrecht." *Germ* XVIII (1873), 110-111.

Sprenger, R., "Zum Meier Helmbrecht." *Germ* XXI (1876), 348-350.

Sprenger, R., "Zum mittelhochdeutschen Wortschatz, rîden, M. H. 264 ff." *Beiträge zur Kunde der idg. Sprachen*, I (1877), 51.

Rudloff, A., *Untersuchungen zu Meier Helmbrecht, von Werner dem Gartenaere.* Rostock, 1878. Dissertation.

REVIEWED: Anon., *JbPh* I (1879), 121.

Birlinger, A., "Nochmal *Giselitze* im Meier Helmbrecht." *Germ* XXV (1880), 432.

Sprenger, R., "Zum Meier Helmbrecht." *Germ* XXV (1880), 407-409.

Inowraclawer, A., *Meier Helmbrecht . . . eine Quelle für deutsche Altertumskunde*. Breslau, 1882. Programm.

REVIEWED: Bechstein, *Lbl* IV (1883), 92.

Seemüller, Josef, "Studien zum kleinen Lucidarius (Seifried Helbling)." *Sitzungsberichte der philosophisch-historischen Classe der kaiserlichen Akademie der Wissenschaften*, Wien, CII (1883), 567-674.

REVIEWED: Schröder, E., *AfdA* X (1884), 56-58.

Müller, Richard, "Beiträge zur Geschichte der mhd. Litteratur in Österreich." *ZfdA* XXXI (1887), 82-103. The discussion of *Meier Helmbrecht* appears as Pt. 2 of the article, pp. 95-103.

Stöwer, W., *Das Kulturhistorische im Meier Helmbrecht*. Bochum, 1891. Programm.

REVIEWED: Anon., *JbPh* XIII (1891), 258; Keinz, *DLZ* XII (1891), 1929; Seemüller, *ZföGy* XLIII (1892), 527; Zingerle, *AfdA* XIX (1893), 297-299.

Sprenger, R., "Zum Meier Helmbrecht." *Germ* XXXVII (1892), 414-415.

Helsig, J., *Metrik und Stilistik im Meier Helmbrecht*. Leipzig, 1892.

Schlickinger, Max, *Der Helmbrechtshof und seine Umgebung*. Eine literarhist. Untersuchung. Linz, 1893. Separatabdruck aus dem 51. *Jahresbericht des Museum Francisco-Carolinum*.

REVIEWED: Anon., *JbPh* XV (1893), 214; Keinz, *AfdA* XX (1894), 258-266; Schlickinger, *ZfdPh* XXIX (1897), 218-223; Löschhorn, *DLZ* XV (1894), 842-843.

Panzer, Fr., "Zum Meier Helmbrecht." *Btr* XXVII (1902), 88-112.

Kraus, C. von, "Zur Kritik des Helmbrecht." *ZfdA* XLVII (1903), 305-318.

REVIEWED: Saran, *JbPh* XXVI (1904), 96 ff.

Schiffmann, K., "Zum Meier Helmbrecht." *ZföGy* LV (1904), 709-718.

REVIEWED: Anon., *JbPh* XXVI (1904), 131-132; Anon., *DLZ* XXV (1904), 3096.

Ehrismann, G., "Über W. Meyers *Fragmenta Burana.*" *ZfdPh* XXXVI (1904), 396 ff. Compares *Ruodlieb* and *Helmbrecht*, pp. 400-401.

Panzer, Fr., "Zum Meier Helmbrecht." *ZfdPh* XXXVIII (1906), 516-518.

Schiffmann, K., "Die Herkunft des Meier Helmbrecht." *Wiener Zeitung*, Nr. 176, 2. Aug., 1907.

Braune, W., "Helmbrechts Haube." *Btr* XXXII (1907), 555-562.

Panzer, Fr., "Zum Meier Helmbrecht." *Btr* XXXIII (1908), 391-398.

Meyer, R. M., "Helmbrecht und seine Haube." *ZfdPh* XL (1908), 421-430.

Haertel, Martin H., "Social Conditions in Southern Bavaria in the 13th Century, as Shown in Meier Helmbrecht." *Transactions of the Wisconsin Acad. of Sciences, Arts and Letters*, XVII (1914), 1057-1072.

Pfannmüller, Ludwig, "Nu zuo des der neve sî! (M. H. 426)." *ZfdA* LV (1914), 278-284.

Schiffmann, K., "Studien zum Helmbrecht." *Btr* XLII (1917), 1-17.
REVIEWED: Anon., *JbPh* XXXVIII (1916), 118-119.

Wilhelm, Fr., "Zur Abfassungszeit des Meier Helmbrecht und des Jüngeren Titurel." *Münchener Museum für Philol. des Mittelalters und der Renaissance*, III (1917-1918), 226-228.
REVIEWED: Anon., *JbPh* XXXIX (1917), 151.

Pfanmüller, Ludwig, "Meier Helmbrecht Studien I, II." *Btr* XL (1918), 252-257; 549-551.
REVIEWED: Anon., *JbPh* XXXIX (1917), 151.

Götze, Alfred, "Zu Wernhers Helmbrecht." *Festschrift Wilhelm Braune* (Aufsätze zur Sprach- und Literaturgeschichte), Dortmund, 1920, pp. 207-210.

Stechele, Karl, "In des Herzogs Stube auf der Burg zu Burghausen." *Das Bayerland*, XXXIII (1921-1922), 344-349.

Kapp, R., *Sind die Rittertreue und der Meier Helmbrecht alternierend abgefasst?* Freiburg, 1922. Typewritten.

Gough, Charles E., "*Ûf rîden* in Meier Helmbrecht, 428." *Mod. Lang. Review*, XVIII (1923), 88-89.

Panzer, Fr., "Zum Meier Helmbrecht." *Btr* XLIX (1924), 142-151.

Wiessner, Edmund, "Helmbrecht und Neidharts Strophen über Hildemar." *Btr* XLIX (1924), 152-158.

Bell, C. H., "Helmbrecht 1251." *Mod. Lang. Notes,* XXXIX (1924), 372-376.

Klibansky, Erich, "Gerichtsszene und Prozessform in erzählenden deutschen Dichtungen des 12.-14. Jh." *Germanische Studien,* XL (1925), 1-64. Pages 57-59: Meier Helmbrecht, von Wernher dem Gärtner.

Gough, C. E., "The Authorship of the Mhg. Poem Meier Helmbrecht." *Proceedings of the Leeds Philos. and Lit. Society,* Literary and Historical Section, I, Pt. 2 (1926), 51-58.

Stechele, K., "Beitrag zur Meier Helmbrecht Forschung." *Altbayrische Monatsschrift,* XV (1926), Heft 3, pp. 25-31.

Gough, C. E., "Notes on the MSS of the Mhg. Poem Meier Helmbrecht." *Proceedings of the Leeds Philos. and Lit. Society,* Literary and Historical Section, I, Pt. 3 (1927), 130-137.

Herbst, K., "Wernher der Gärtner: Meier Helmbrecht, eine Dorfgeschichte." *Zeitschrift für deutsches ländliches Fortbildungsschulwesen in Preussen,* 1928, pp. 650-658.

## GENERAL LITERATURE

Schröder, Carl, "Die höfische Dorfpoesie des deutschen Mittelalters." Gosches *Jahrbuch für Literaturgeschichte,* I (1865), 45-98. Pages 52-64: *Meier Helmbrecht.*

Schultz, Alwin, *Das höfische Leben zur Zeit der Minnesänger.* Leipzig, 1879.

Goedeke, Karl, *Grundriss zur Geschichte der deutschen Dichtung, aus den Quellen.* 2. Aufl., Dresden, 1884. I, 112-113.

Fränkel, L., *Allgemeine deutsche Biographie.* Leipzig, XLII (1897), 77-80: "Wernher der Gartenaere (Gärtner)."

Hagelstange, Alfred, *Süddeutsches Bauernleben im Mittelalter.* Leipzig, 1898.

Grimm, J., *Deutsche Rechtsaltertümer.* Leipzig, 1899.

Bernays, Michael, "Zur neuesten Litteratur." *Schriften zur Kritik und Litteraturgeschichte,* hrsg. von Geo. Witkowski. Berlin, 1899. IV, 164-170.

Coulton, G. G., *The Medieval Village.* Cambridge, 1925.

Hügli, H., "*Der deutsche Bauer im Mittelalter,* dargestellt nach den deutschen literarischen Quellen vom 11.-15. Jh."

Bern, 1929. *Sprache und Dichtung, Forschungen zur Sprach- und Literaturwissenschaft*, hrsg. von H. Maync und S. Singer. H. 42. Contains a good bibliography of general literature, pp. 174-176.

## II. DER ARME HEINRICH

### MANUSCRIPTS

Hartmann von Aue's *Der arme Heinrich* is preserved in two versions, A and B, the latter of which — the inferior version — is extant in two copies, Bᵃ and Bᵇ. In addition, there are fragments of two other MSS, designated as C and D. See Gierach, *Der arme Heinrich*, pp. vii-ix, and Ehrismann, *Geschichte der deutschen Literature*, p. 197.

A. Strassburg MS, 14th century (burned in 1870).

Bᵃ. Heidelberg MS, 14th century.

Bᵇ. Kalocza (Hungary) MS, 14th century.

C. St. Florian Fragments, 13th century.

D. Indersdorf Fragments, 14th century.

### MIDDLE HIGH GERMAN EDITIONS

*Sammlung deutscher Gedichte aus dem 12., 13., und 14. Jh.*, hrsg. von Christoph H. Myller (Müller). Berlin, 1784. Bd. I, 197-208: *Der arme Heinrich.* A print of MS A, from a copy made by Breitinger.

*Kaloczaer Kodex altdeutscher Gedichte*, hrsg. von Johann N. Graf Mailáth und Johann P. Köffinger. Pest, 1817. Pages 421-464: *Der arme Heinrich.* A print of MS Bᵇ.

*Der arme Heinrich, von Hartmann von der Aue.* Aus der strassburgischen und vatikanischen [Bᵃ] Handschrift hrsg. und erklärt durch die Brüder Grimm. Berlin, 1815.

*Auswahl aus den hochdeutschen Dichtern des 13. Jh.*, von Karl Lachmann. Berlin, 1820. Pages 1-52: *Von dem armen Heinrich.* 5. Aufl., 1873.

*Deutsches Lesebuch*, von Wilhelm Wackernagel. Basel, 1835. 1. Teil, *Altdeutsches Lesebuch.* Poesie und Prosa vom IV. bis bum XV. Jh. Pages 523-562: *Der arme Heinrich.* 6. Aufl., 1873.

*Der arme Heinrich, von Hartmann von Aue.* Zu Vorlesungen und zum Schulgebrauch mit einem Wörterbuch hrsg. von Wilhelm Müller. Göttingen, 1842. 2. Aufl., 1881.

*Die Lieder und Büchlein und der Arme Heinrich, von Hart-*

*mann von Aue*, hrsg. von Moriz Haupt. Leipzig, 1842.
Pages 111-172: *Der arme Heinrich*. 2. Aufl., besorgt von
E. Martin, Leipzig, 1881.

REVIEWED: Anon., *JbPh* III (1881), 131; Sauer, *ZföGy* XXXII
(1881), 917-918; Behagel, *Lbl* II (1881), Nr. 12, p. 427; Roediger,
*DLZ* III (1882), 534-535; Anon., *LCbl* XLVII (1882), 1593-
1594.

REPRINTED:

*Der arme Heinrich, von Hartmann von Aue*, hrsg. von T. G. Karajan. Wien, 1850. With corrections.

*Edelsteine deutscher Dichtung und Weisheit im 13. Jh.*, hrsg. von
Philipp Wackernagel. Frankfurt, Erlangen, 1850; 2. Aufl., 1857.

*Altdeutsche Sprachproben*, hrsg. von Karl Müllenhoff. Berlin, 1864;
3. Aufl., 1878; 4. Aufl., besorgt von Rödiger, 1885. *Der arme Heinrich* appears first in the 3. Aufl., pp. 136-152.

*Herr Hartmann von Owe. Diu maere vom armen Heinrich*. Hrsg.
von H[einrich] W[ansleben]. Kiel, Lipsius u. Fischer, 1880. A
lithographed text, in the form of an old 12th-century MS. After P.
Wackernagel, *Edelsteine deutscher Dichtung*.

ANNOUNCEMENT, with brief critical remarks: Anon., *Lbl* I
(1881), 33.

*Altdeutsches Lesebuch für höhere Lehranstalten*, hrsg. von
August Henneberger. Halle, 1849. Pages 103-127: *Der
arme Heinrich*.

*Der arme Heinrich Herrn Hartmanns von Aue und zwei jün-
gere Prosalegenden verwandten Inhalts*, hrsg. von Wilhelm
Wackernagel. Basel, 1855.

REVIEWED: Pfeiffer, *Germ* I (1856), 126-128.

REPRINTED:

Mit Anmerkungen und Abhandlungen von Wilh. Wackernagel.
Hrsg. von Wilh. Toischer. Basel, 1885.

REVIEWED: Anon., *JbPh* VII (1885), 182-183; Behagel, *Lbl* VI
(1885), 279-280; Burdach, *AfdA* XII (1886), 189-200; Koch,
*Grenzboten* XLIV (1885), 403-408; Martin, *DLZ* VI (1885),
1109-1110; Hruschka, *ZföRealschulen*, X (1885), 171.

Neu hrsg. von Ernst Stadler. Basel, 1911.

REVIEWED: Schröder, *AfdA* XXXV (1912), 278-279; Leitzmann,
*ZfdPh* XLIV (1912), 369-370; Ehrismann, *Lbl* XXXIV (1913),
320-321.

*Hartmann von Aue*, hrsg. von Fedor Bech. Leipzig, 1867.
Bd. 4-6, *Deutsche Klassiker des Mittelalters*. 2. Teil (Bd.
5), 285 ff.: *Der arme Heinrich*. 3. Aufl., 1891.

REVIEWED: Anon., *JbPh* XIII (1891), 248.

*Sechs Lieder und Der arme Heinrich Hartmanns von Aue*,

hrsg. und mit Anmerkungen und einem Glossar versehen, von Bernhard Schulz. Leipzig, 1871. Pages 9-61.

*Die Werke Hartmanns von Aue. Altdeutsche Textbibliothek,* Bd. II-III, hrsg. von Hermann Paul. Halle, 1882. Bd. III: *Der arme Heinrich.* 7. Aufl., besorgt von Albert Lutzmann, 1930.

REVIEWED: Toischer, *Lbl* III (1882), 453-455; Anon., *LCbl* 1882, pp. 1264-1265.

*Höfische Epik.* Bearbeitet von Paul Piper. Stuttgart, 1889. II. Teil: *Hartmann von Aue und seine Nachahmer. Deutsche National-Litteratur,* hrsg. von Jos. Kürschner. IV Bd., Erste Abt., 2. Pages 86-123: *Der arme Heinrich.*

*Der arme Heinrich, by Hartmann von Aue,* ed. with an introd., notes and glossary by John G. Robertson. London, 1895. With facsimile. Based on Paul, with changes after Haupt and Wackernagel.

REVIEWED: Collins, *Mod. Lang. Notes,* XII (1897), 186-188; Jonas, *Mod. Lang. Notes,* XVII (1902), 294-300.

*Hartmann von Aue (Der arme Heinrich), Wolfram von Eschenbach (Parzival) und Gottfried von Strassburg (Tristan).* Eine Auswahl aus dem höfischen Epos mit Anmerkungen und Wörterbuch, von Karl Marold. Stuttgart, 1892. *Sammlung Göschen,* Bd. 22. 3. Aufl., besorgt von H[ermann] Jantzen, Berlin, 1920.

*Parzival, Der arme Heinrich, Walter von der Vogelweide* . . . Erläuterungen. Für den Schulgebrauch hrsg. von Wilh. Stein. Habelschwerdt, 1909.

*Der arme Heinrich, von Hartmann von Aue.* Überlieferung und Herstellung. Hrsg. von Erich Gierach. Heidelberg, 1913. Streitbergs *Germanische Bibliothek.* Abt. 3, Kritische Ausgaben altdeutscher Texte. Hrsg. von C. v. Kraus und K. Zwierzina. Bd. III.

REVIEWED: Anon., *JbPh* XXXV (1913), 123; Piquet, *RC* LXXVI (1913), 513; Mensel, *JEGPh* XIV (1915), 121-123; Helm, *Lbl* XXXVI (1915), 325-326; Oehl, *Allg. Lbl* XXV (1916), 177.

2. Aufl., 1925.

REVIEWED: Schröder, *AfdA* XLV (1926), 39-40.

*Hartmann von Aue: Der arme Heinrich.* Für die Schule bearbeitet von Franz J. Prohaska-Hotze. Wien, 1925. *Deutsche Bücherei für mittl. Lehranstalten.*

*Hartmann von Aue: Der arme Heinrich.* Leipzig, Insel Verlag, 1925.

*Hartmann von Aue: Der arme Heinrich.* Hrsg. v. M. M.

Annuntiata Küpper. Paderborn [1926]. Ferd. Schöninghs *Dombücherei*, H. 31. Mhd. Ausgabe, mit eingelegtem nhd. Text. Schulausgabe.

*Der arme Heinrich.* In *Mittelhochdeutsches Lesebuch.* . . . Hrsg. von Gust. Legerlotz. 3. Aufl., 1905. Velhagen und Klasings *Sammlung deutscher Schulausgaben,* hrsg. von J. Wychgram. Bd. 62, pp. 90-98.

## MODERN GERMAN METRICAL TRANSLATIONS

*Der arme Heinrich.* Eine altdeutsche Erzählung. Hrsg. von J. G. G. Büsching. Zürich, 1810. Mit Kupfern von Franz Hegi.

REVIEWED: J. Grimm, *Heidelberger Jahrbücher,* 5. Jahrgang, 1. Hälfte (1812), 49-57; W. Grimm, *Kleinere Schriften,* VI, 64-70.

REPRINTED IN:

*Deutsche Anthologie oder Blumenlese aus den Klassikern der Deutschen,* von Friedrich Rassman. Zwickau, 1821. Pages 97-162.

*Hartmann von Aue: Der arme Heinrich,* übersetzt von K. Simrock. Berlin, 1830. In *Althochdeutsches Lesebuch in neuhochdeutscher Sprache,* 1854, pp. 261 ff. 2. Aufl., Heilbronn, 1875, pp. 85 ff.

ED. OF 1830 REVIEWED: W. Grimm, *Kleinere Schriften,* Bd. II, 426-427.

*Der arme Heinrich,* von Adalbert v. Chamisso. Deutsches Musenalmanach, 1839, pp. 7-26. In Chamisso's *Werke,* hrsg. von Tardel, 1907, Bd. I, 257-269. A shortened version.

*Der arme Heinrich.* Nach Hartmann von Aue. Mit fünf Holzschnitten. Hrsg. von G. O. Marbach. Leipzig [1842]. *Volksbücher,* 32.

*Das Ritterbuch,* hrsg. von Fr. Koch. Halle, 1848. I: *Hartmanns von Aue Iwein und Der arme Heinrich.*

*Der arme Heinrich, von Hartmann von der Aue.* Aus dem Mhd. übersetzt von Hans von Wolzogen. Leipzig, 1872. Reclam, Nr. 456.

*Der arme Heinrich, von Hartmann von Aue.* Poetische Erzählung aus dem 13. Jh. Übertragen, bearb. und den deutschen Jungfrauen gewidmet von G. Hausmann. Gotha, 1886.

*Hartmann von der Aue: Der arme Heinrich.* Neuhochdeutsch bearbeitet von Th. Ebner. Halle, 1887. *Bibliothek der Gesamt-Lit. des In- und Auslandes,* Nr. 84.

*Denkmäler der älteren deutschen Litteratur* . . . hrsg. von

G. Bötticher und K. Kinzel. Halle, 1891. II, Die höfische Dichtung des Mittelalters, 2: *Der arme Heinrich*, nebst dem Inhalte des *Erek* und *Iwein* von Hartmann von Aue und *Meier Helmbrecht* von Wernher dem Gärtner, übersetzt und erläutert von Gotthold Bötticher.

REVIEWED: Erdmann, *ZfdPh* XXIV (1892), 139-140.

2. Aufl., 1899.

REVIEWED: Wetzel, *ZföGy* LIII (1899), 709-710.

9. Aufl., 1925.

*Der arme Heinrich, von Hartmann von Aue.* Übersetzt und bearbeitet von G. Bornhak. Leipzig, 1892. Teubners *Sammlung deutscher Dicht- und Schriftwerke für höhere Töchterschulen*, Nr. 24.

REVIEWED: Anon., *JbPh* XIV (1892), 228, 242.

*Der arme Heinrich.* Eine schwäbische Sage. Aus dem Mhd. übertragen von Aug. Hagedorn. Leipzig, 1898.

REVIEWED: Anon., *JbPh* XX (1898), 90.

*Hartmann von Aue: Epik der deutschen Sagenkreise.* Übertr. und eingeleitet von Gustav Legerlotz. Bielefeld, Leipzig, 1904. Pages 1-44: *Der arme Heinrich.* Velhagen und Klasings *Sammlung deutscher Schulausgaben*, Nr. 107.

*Hartmann von Aue: Lieder, Der arme Heinrich.* Neudeutsch von Will Vesper. München, 1905. *Statuen deutscher Kultur*, Bd. II.

*Aus deutscher Vorzeit.* Mit einem Anhang: Hartmann von Aue, *Der arme Heinrich.* Neu übersetzt von Elly Steffen. Grössenwörden [1907]. *Deutsche Bücherei*, Bd. 86/87.

*Hartmann von Aue: Der arme Heinrich.* Sprachlich erneuert von Otto Hauser. Weimar, 1922. *Aus deutschen Gärten*, Nr. 10.

*Hartmann von Aue, Der arme Heinrich.* Besorgt von Rudolf Borchardt. München, 1925. Written in archaic language which is only a slight modernization of the Middle High German. Similar in style to Borchart's translation of Dante.

*Der arme Heinrich, von Hartmann von Aue.* In die Sprache der Gegenwart übertragen von A. Eckhart. Bühl [1927].

*Der arme Heinrich.* Nach der Dichtung Hartmanns von Aue frei übertragen von Bernhard Oest. Frankfurt, 1929. *Kranz-Bücherei*, H. 93. Mit Titelbild.

MODERN GERMAN PROSE TRANSLATIONS

*Der arme Heinrich* [translated by Wilhelm Grimm. In the

M. H. G. edition] *Der arme Heinrich, von Hartmann von der Aue.* Aus der strassburgischen und vatikanischen [B<sup>a</sup>] Handschrift hrsg. und erklärt durch die Brüder Grimm. Berlin, 1815, pp. 1-30.

REPRINTED:

*Waltharilied, Der arme Heinrich, Lieder der alten Edda,* übersetzt von den Brüdern Grimm. Mit Buchschmuck von E. Liebermann. Hamburg, 1905.

REVIEWED: Bernt, *ZföGy* LVII (1906), 218-219.

*Wilhelm Grimm: Deutsche Sagen.* Wiesbaden, 1906. *Wiesbadener Volksbücher,* Nr. 51. Pages 29-54: *Der arme Heinrich.*

*Hartmann von Aue: Der arme Heinrich,* übertr. von Wilh. Grimm. Mit 4 farb. Tafeln. Dachau [1920]. *Einhorn Drucke,* Bd. 4.

*Hartmann von Aue: Der arme Heinrich,* übertr. von Wilh. Grimm. Farbige Holzschnitte von Willi Harwerth. Offenbach, 1924.

*Buch der schönsten Geschichten und Sagen,* hrsg. von Gustav Schwab. Stuttgart, 1836. I. Teil, *Der arme Heinrich.* 2. Aufl., Stuttgart, 1843.

THIS BECOMES: *Die deutschen Volksbücher,* für Jung und Alt wieder erzählt von Gustav Schwab. 4. Aufl., Stuttgart, 1859. Pages 75-90: *Der arme Heinrich.* Mit Illustrationen nach Adolf Ehrhardt. Neu durchgesehen von J. Mayer. Reutlingen [1905].

*Die deutschen Volksbücher,* gesammelt und in ihrer ursprünglichen Echtheit wiederhergestellt von Karl Simrock. Frankfurt, 1847. VI, 171-203: *Der arme Heinrich.* Two woodcuts.

*Der arme Heinrich, von Hartmann von Aue. Mit sieben Zeichnungen.* Josef von Führich. Leipzig, 1878.

*Das Übersetzen aus dem Mittelhochdeutschen,* von Franz Saran. Halle, 1930. Pages 39-76: *Der arme Heinrich.* A model prose translation.

## DRAMATIZATIONS[1]

[*Der arme Heinrich*], by Ludwig Uhland. 1818. In *Uhland als Dramatiker,* von Adalb. von Keller, Stuttgart, 1877, pp. 407-409. A dramatic fragment of 24 verses without title.

*Der arme Heinrich.* Schauspiel in einem Aufzuge nach einem

---

[1] Tardel ("Der arme Heinrich," *Forschungen zur neueren Literaturgeschichte,* XXX, p. 18) records an unprinted play *Der arme Heinrich* von Gustav Gugitz, Wien. He also reports that the play *Der arme Heinrich* von Ludwig Heller, staged in Nürnberg March 1902, is only loosely connected with the Hartmann material, and that the two-act comedy *Der arme Heinrich* von Franz Bonn, München, 1880, is entirely unrelated.

altdeutschen Gedicht, von K. Ludw. Kannegiesser. Zwickau, 1836.

*Heinrich von der Aue.* Schauspiel in vier Aufzügen, von Josef Weilen. Leipzig, 1874. Reclam, Nr. 570.

*Der arme Heinrich*, von Anonyma. Hamburg, 1861.

*Verwundet und geheilt.* Dramatisches Gedicht in fünf Aufzügen, von Betty Fischer (Pseudonym: E. Rutenberg). Freiburg im Breisgau, 1881.

*Der arme Heinrich.* Deutsches Volksbühnenspiel von Hans Pöhnl. Wien, 1887.

*Der arme Heinrich.* Ein deutsches Volksschauspiel in fünf Abteilungen, von Carl Schultes. Leipzig, 1894.

*Der arme Heinrich.* Drama in vier Aufzügen, von Hermann Hanau. Berlin, 1900.

*Der arme Heinrich.* Schauspiel in sechs Bildern, von Käthe Becher (Pseudonym: Hans Erdmann). Berlin, 1900.

*San Marcos Tochter.* Romantisches Trauerspiel, von Arthur Fitger. Oldenburg, 1902.

*Der arme Heinrich.* Eine deutsche Sage in fünf Akten, von Gerhart Hauptmann. 1902. In *Gesammelte Werke*, Jubiläumsausgabe, Berlin [no date], III, 263-373.

REVIEWED: Lorenz, *Preussische Jahrbücher*, CXI (1903), 166; E. Stilgebauer, "Hartmanns und Hauptmanns Armer Heinrich," *Zur Guten Stunde*, XXXI (1903), 18-20. Cf. Krumpelmann, *infra*.

*Der arme Heinrich*, von Ernst Hammer. Kiel, 1905.

## OTHER LITERARY TREATMENTS

*Henry the Leper.* A Swabian Miracle-Rhyme. By Dante Gabriel Rossetti. 1846-1847. In *Collected Works*, London, 1897, II, 420-460.

*The Golden Legend*, by Henry Wadsworth Longfellow. 1851. In *Poetical Works*, Riverside ed., 1890, V, 139-292.

TREATMENTS:

F. Münzner: *Die Quellen zu Longfellows Golden Legend*. Programm. Dresden, 1898. Nr. 589. Festschrift der 44. Versammlung deutscher Philologen, pp. 249-285.

Jenny Wieruszowski: "Der arme Heinrich bei Longfellow." *Das literarische Echo*, V (1903), 930-931.

John T. Krumpelmann: "Longfellow's *Golden Legend* and the *Armer Heinrich* theme in modern German literature." *JEGPh* XXV (1926), 173-192.

TRANSLATIONS INTO GERMAN:

*Die goldene Legende,* Deutsch von Karl Keck. Leipzig, 1860.

*Die goldene Legende,* übers. von Elise Freifrau von Hohenhausen. Leipzig, 1880; 2. Aufl., 1882.

*Die goldene Legende,* übers. von P. Kaegler. Halle [no date], *Hendelsche Bibliothek.*

*Die goldene Legende.* In *Longfellows sämtliche poetische Werke,* übers. von Hermann Simon. Leipzig, 1883. Reclam, *Helios-Klassiker.*

*The Golden Legend of Poor Henry,* translated from the German of Hartmann von der Aue, a poet of the thirteenth century, for the *Republican,* by A. E. Kroeger. *Missouri Republican* (daily), Dec. 25, 1869. A fragment.

*Dal tedesco medioevale. Il povero Enrico.* Versione in prosa, di Aristide Baragiola. Strassburg, 1881.

REVIEWED: Martin, *AfdA* VIII (1882), 169-170.

*A beteg Henrik,* Költöi elbeszélés a XIII század ból. Irta: Hartmann von Aue. N. E. Vende. Budapest, 1893. Magyar (*Der arme Heinrich,* poetische Erzählung aus dem 13. Jh. Programm).

REVIEWED: Petz, *Egyetemes philologiai közlöny* (1893), 227-229.

*Der arme Heinrich.* Opera. Hans Pfitzner [Komponist], James Grum [Textdichter]. 1895.

REVIEWED: Batka, *Kunstwart,* XIII, I. Hälfte (1899), 51-54.

*Der arme Heinrich,* von Ricarda Huch. In *Fra Celeste und andere Erzählungen,* pp. 89-203. Leipzig, 1899. A story in a collection of stories.

*Der arme Heinrich, von Hartmann von Aue,* in ahd. blankverse übertragen von H. Paul. Linz, 1906. Programm.

CRITICAL LITERATURE[2]

Schönbach, A. E., *Über Hartmann von Aue.* Drei Bücher Untersuchungen. Graz, 1894.

Piquet, F., *Étude sur Hartmann d'Aue.* Paris, 1898.

Jellinek, A. L., "Der arme Heinrich im Drama." *Das lit. Echo,* V (1903), 1371.

Meyer, R. M., "Zur Geschichte des Armen Heinrich." *Die Zeit* (Wien), XXXV (1903), 130-132; (1904), 454.

---

[2] In view of the exhaustive bibliographical references contained in Ehrismann, *Geschichte der deutschen Literatur,* only a few essential references are listed here. For general literature, see the references in the Helmbrecht bibliography above.

Nestle, "Die Miselsucht." *Zeitschrift für den deutschen Unterricht*, XVIII (1904), 66-67.

Tardel, H., "Der arme Heinrich in der neueren Dichtung." *Forschungen zur neueren Literaturgeschichte*, XXX. Berlin, 1905.

Ehrismann, Gustav, *Geschichte der deutschen Literatur bis zum Ausgang des Mittelalters*. München, 1927. 2. Teil: *Die mhd. Literatur*. II Blütezeit, 1. Hälfte. Pages 141-212: *Hartmann von Aue*. The most recent scholarly treatment, with exhaustive bibliographical references.

Kraus, Carl von, "Drei Märlein in der Parzifalhandschrift G und das Exempel vom Armen Heinrich." In *Festgabe für Samuel Singer*, hrsg. von Harry Maync. Tübingen, 1930, pp. 1-19.

Kraus, Carl von, "Drei Märlein in der Parzifalhandschrift G und das Exempel vom Armen Heinrich." *Forschungen und Fortschritte, Nachrichtenblatt der deutschen Wissenschaft und Technik*, VI (1930), 447.

Sparnay, H., "Die Einstellung des Armen Heinrichs in das Werk Hartmanns von Aue." *ZfdA* LXVII (1930), 23-41.

# INDEX

# INDEX

Hen, *see* Chicken
Henneberger, p. 164
Herbort von Fritzlar, p. 138 n. 5
Herbst, p. 162
Herzog Ernst (II), M. H., vs. 957; p. 140 n. 33
Hired help, M. H., vs. 711; p. 140 n. 26
Hoffmann, p. 159
Hofmiller, pp. 21, 158
*Hofzucht*, p. 141 n. 34
Hohenhausen, p. 170
Hohenstein, p. 10; M. H., vs. 192
Höllensack, M. H., vs. 1189
  meaning, p. 141 n. 35
Homer, p. 137 n. 3
Hood, *see* Clothing (male)
Horse, M. H., vss. 235 ff., 369 ff., 387, 394 ff., 457, 670, 760, 843, 1210, 1780; A. H., vss. 781, 1022; *see also* Colt, Stallion
Hruschka, p. 164
Huch, p. 170
Hügli, pp. 5, 6, 16, 18, 139 n. 20, 145 n. 13, 146 n. 28, 149, 162
Hunting, M. H., vss. 986 ff.

*Iliad*, pp. 17, 137 n. 3
Implements, *see* Accountrements; Farm implements
Inheritance of characteristics from godfather, M. H., vss. 480 ff., 1379 ff.; p. 139 n. 21
Inn River, p. 139 n. 23
Inowraclawer, pp. 149, 160
*Isolt* (safe box), p. 141 n. 36
*Iwein*, pp. 23, 24, 25

*Jakobsbrüder*, p. 25
Jänicke, p. 159
Jantzen, p. 165
Jellinek, p. 170
Job, A. H., vss. 130, 138 ff.
Jonas, p. 165
Jousts, M. H., vss. 1023 ff.
Judge
  bribing of, M. H., vss. 1673 ff.
  right to unclaimed stolen goods, M. H., vs. 1668; p. 143 n. 53

*Jüngere Titurel, Der*, p. 138 n. 7, 142

Kaegler, p. 170
Kaiser, M. H., vs. 411
*Kaiserchronik*, pp. 6, 25, 138 n. 9
Kannegiesser, p. 169
Kapp, p. 161
Karajan, p. 164
Keck, p. 170
Keinz, pp. 9, 10, 19, 20, 137 n. 4, 138 n. 10, 139 n. 16, n. 23, 140 n. 31, 141 n. 36, 142 n. 42, 143 n. 49, 155, 159, 160
Kid, M. H., vs. 674
King Arthur, M. H., vs. 1478; p. 142 n. 46
Kinzel, pp. 156, 157, 167
Kistener, p. 25
Klee, p. 156
*Kleine Lucidarius, Der*, see *Seifried Helbling*
Klibansky, pp. 143 n. 52, n. 54; 162
Knife, doctor's, A. H., vs. 1209
Knight, *see also* Robber knight
  as composer of minnesongs, A. H., vs. 71; p. 144 n. 3
  reading ability rare, A. H., vss. 1 ff.; p. 144 n. 1
Knighthood, M. H., vss. 986 ff.; *see also* Accountrements; Archery; Dancing; Hunting; Jousts; Minstrelsy; Tournaments
  decay of, pp. 4 ff.; M. H., vss. 984 ff.
  in its prime, M. H., vss. 913 ff.
Koch, pp. 164, 166
Köffinger, p. 163
Konrad von Würzburg, pp. 25, 27, 138 n. 5
*Kräpfen*, p. 150
Kraus, pp. 26, 160, 165, 171
Kraut, *Privatrecht*, p. 146 n. 28
Kraut, M. H., vss. 867, 1604; p. 140 n. 31
Kroeger, pp. 29, 170
Krumpelmann, p. 169
Kuhfrass, M. H., vs. 1191
  meaning, p. 141 n. 35

# RECORDS OF CIVILIZATION
## SOURCES AND STUDIES

Edited under the auspices of the
### Department of History, Columbia University

A series of volumes containing documents in translation, commentaries and inter-
pretations, and bibliographical guides. (Uniform in size and binding, octavo,
cloth, stamped in gold.)

## PUBLISHED VOLUMES

## COLUMBIA UNIVERSITY PRESS
### COLUMBIA UNIVERSITY
#### NEW YORK

FOREIGN AGENT
OXFORD UNIVERSITY PRESS
HUMPHREY MILFORD
AMEN HOUSE, LONDON, E. C.

# RECORDS OF CIVILIZATION

## SOURCES AND STUDIES

## COLUMBIA UNIVERSITY PRESS

### COLUMBIA UNIVERSITY

NEW YORK

FOREIGN AGENT
OXFORD UNIVERSITY PRESS
HUMPHREY MILFORD
AMEN HOUSE, LONDON, E. C.